New Edition

Viewfinder

Topics

Politics in the U.S.A.

We the People ...

compiled and edited by
Reimer Jansen, Cornelia Becker and Ulrich Imig

In memory of Henning Scholz

L

Langenscheidt

Berlin · München · Wien · Zürich · New York

Viewfinder

Topics

Unterrichtsmaterialien für die Sekundarstufe II

Politics in the U.S.A.

We the People ...

Herausgeber:
Prof. em. Dr. Dr. h.c. Dr. h.c. Peter Freese, Paderborn

Autoren:
Reimer Jansen, Cornelia Becker, Ulrich Imig

Projekt-Team:
Dr. Martin Arndt, Münster
David Beal, M. A., Bochum
Cornelia Becker, Bremen
Dr. Peter Dines, Cert. Ed., Ludwigsburg
Prof. i. R. Dr. Hanspeter Dörfel, Ludwigsburg
OStR Dieter Düwel, Castrop-Rauxel
Prof. em. Dr. Dr. h.c. Dr. h.c. Peter Freese, Paderborn
Dr. Carin Freywald †
Jennifer von der Grün, B. A., Castrop-Rauxel
OStR Ulrich Imig, Wildeshausen
OStR Reimer Jansen, Oyten-Sagehorn
Dr. Michael Mitchell, M. A., Reken und Warwick
Prof. Dr. Michael Porsche, Paderborn
StD i. E. Detlef Rediker, Lippstadt
StD Dr. Peter-J. Rekowski, Kirchhain
OStR i.K. Peter Ringeisen, M. A., Amberg
Karl Sassenberg, Münster
StD Henning Scholz †
StR Dr. Annegret Schrick, Gevelsberg
OStR Ekkehard Sprenger, Olympia, USA
OStD Dr. Dietrich Theißen, Gütersloh
Donald Turner, M. A. †
Prof. Dr. Laurenz Volkmann, Jena
Philip Wade, M. A., Cert. Ed., Amberg

Verlagsredaktion: Dr. Beatrix Finke
Layout und Produktion: Barbara Slowik, Atelier S., München

www.langenscheidt.de/viewfinder

Umwelthinweis: Gedruckt auf chlorfrei gebleichtem Papier.

1. Auflage 2006

© 2006 Langenscheidt KG, Berlin und München

Druck: Druckhaus Berlin-Mitte GmbH, Berlin
Printed in Germany

ISBN 13: 978-3-526-51010-9
ISBN 10: 3-526-51010-5

1 2 3 4 5 / 10 09 08 07 06

Contents

Politics in the U.S.A. (Collage) .... p. 4

1 | John Locke: *The Second Treatise of Government* (1690) .... p. 6

2 | "We the People of the United States" .... p. 8

3 | Peter Vilbig, Stacey Delikat: "Enough is Enough" .... p. 12

4 | Peter Bromhead: "The Parties" .... p. 15

5 | Dudley Buffa: "The Future of American Democracy"* .... p. 18

6 | "Federal Government" .... p. 20

7 | Dirk Johnson: "A Nation Bound by Faith" .... p. 23
    Info: The Relationship between Church and State .... p. 25
    Info: Pledge of Allegiance .... p. 26

8 | Joanne M. Marshall: "Religion and Education:
   Walking the Line in Public Schools" .... p. 27

9 | Art Buchwald: "School Prayers" .... p. 28

10 | Dean A. Murphy: "Imagining America without Illegal Immigrants" .... p. 30
    Info: Where Illegal Immigrants Come From .... p. 32
    Info: The United States Immigration and Naturalization Service .... p. 33

11 | Shannon Brownlee: "The Overtreated American" .... p. 34

12 | Karen Kornbluh: "The Parent Trap" .... p. 37

13 | Jennifer Washburn: "The Tuition Crunch" .... p. 40

14 | "The Economy/International Trade" .... p. 42

15 | Andrew C. Revkin: "The Heat Is On" .... p. 44

16 | David Lehman: "The World Trade Center" .... p. 48

   Andrea Carter Brown: "The Old Neighborhood" .... p. 50

17 | *Statement from American Scholars*
   Supporting the U. S. Government's War on Terrorism .... p. 52

   Noam Chomsky: "Reflections on 9-11" .... p. 54
    Info: Just War .... p. 56

18 | Michael Hirsh: "We Were Wrong" .... p. 57
    Info: American Foreign Policy .... p. 59
    Info: Vietnam War (1954-1975) .... p. 60

19 | John Maggs: "Too Much Like Vietnam" .... p. 61

* Title provided by the editors

Politics in the U.S.A.

In 1982, Klaus Harpprecht published a book on the United States of America based on his experience as a film-producer and journalist in this country. Its title was: *Der fremde Freund*, which expresses in a nutshell why it is important and rewarding to analyze and understand U.S.-American politics.

Since the end of World War II, the relationship, based on shared values, has been very firm between the Federal Republic of Germany and the United States of America . Yet, it has always been dynamic. In spite of the fact that Germany has been one of the most loyal allies for a long time, there have been periods of misunderstanding, minor tensions and discord. Chancellor Schröder's (1998 - 2005) clear stance against the military intervention in Iraq in 2003 caused the most recent strain on the German-American relationship.

However, it should not be forgotten that Germany has been participating in *Operation Enduring Freedom*, the U.S. military operation launched in 2001, against the Taliban regime in Afghanistan. In January 2006, Angela Merkel made her first visit to Washington, D.C., as the new Chancellor of the Federal Republic. The exchange of opinions – despite some differences with President George W. Bush on crucial issues – was unanimously evaluated as the beginning of a new chapter in U.S.-American / German post-war relations. Gaining insight into American politics helps to provide for intercultural understanding. Presenting developments, issues, and mechanisms of U.S. society and its political institutions in a cultural and historical context may help to prevent naive anti-Americanism as well as an uncritical admiration of American ways.

The following outline may help to give an introduction into the main features of *Politics in the U.S.A.*:
• Firstly, texts about the genesis and the content of the **Constitution** emphasize the philosophical ideas of the Age of Enlightenment as the main source of the U.S.-American democracy as a model for modern democracies. The Constitution, based on the principles of *Separation of Powers* and *Checks and Balances* and its *Amendments* (with the first ten amendments constituting *The Bill of Rights*) guarantees the system and spirit of a workable and adaptable **Democracy in Action**.
• Secondly, the importance of **Religion** in the United States of America, the ostentatious demonstration of piety, the religious and moral attitudes frequently expressed in political speeches and determining decisions and - at the same time - the emphasis on the constitutionally established dividing line between Church and State, the exact definition of which repeatedly is the central issue of numerous Supreme Court cases, seems to be a paradox to a lot of European observers. These phenomena have to be explained in a wider historical and social context to understand certain facets of U.S. domestic and foreign policies.
• Thirdly, information on challenges in such fields as **Social Policy**, **Education**, the relationship between **Ecology and Economy** sketches the issues at stake predominantly in domestic affairs, normally not so thoroughly covered by the media as other political topics. These challenges and the solutions discussed by experts and political leaders are necessary to understand the U.S.A. However short-lived some of the dates and figures offered in the texts may be (they can easily be updated with the help of official

websites, e.g. www.usembassy.de) - the issues allow insights into the more lasting principles of pragmatic political thought. Besides, the topics of home affairs invite comparison to current problems and issues in Germany and other countries within the European Union at a time in which economic and social reforms are urgently needed.

• Fourthly, throughout history, America has perceived itself as a nation of **Immigrants**. This aspect has led to challenges and controversies concerning the structure of American society up to the present day. The never-ending debates on assimilation versus diversity, the current socio-economic issue of the status of illegal immigrants and the development of a new immigration legislation prove this fact.

• Fifthly, **Terrorism**, above all, the atrocities of 9/11, brought about a paradigmatic change in U.S.-American politics. Apart from such reactions as shock, fear, and measures dictated by the priority of home security, the terrorist attacks initiated fundamental reflections on U.S.-American identity and values. Famous U.S.-American scholars re-examined and reaffirmed the validity of the United States' values and human rights in a style reminiscent of classical political writing in the Age of Enlightenment before they justified *the War on Terrorism*. The apology of defense measures went hand in hand with self-critical explanations why something like 9/11 had happened. More radical self-criticism of the American way of life and the nation's foreign policy blend in with the general criticism of the globalization process. For outside observers of politics in the United States it is important to see that much of their own critical reactions to the U.S.-American administration's decisions are expressed in open, controversial debates within the United States of America itself. This holds also true for the assessment and reassessment of America's military commitments due to its changing **Global Role** as a superpower such as the Vietnam War and the military operation in Iraq of 2003.

We the People ...

1 John Locke

The Second Treatise of Government (1690)

Many people believe that the French Revolution of 1789 was the first great movement towards democracy in the western world. But they are wrong, because the American Declaration of Independence was published thirteen years earlier and laid the foundation of a new democratic state that was to become the model of many other democracies. But the ideas that led the authors to such a revolutionary act had already been conceived and expressed more than eighty years earlier by the philosophers of the late seventeenth and the eighteenth centuries. Among the British philosophers of that epoch are best known Thomas Hobbes and John Locke. Especially John Locke's "Second Treatise of Government" had an enormous influence on the leading thinkers of the American Colonies. - John Locke, *The Second Treatise of Government* (1690), (New York: The Liberal Arts Press, 1952), pp. 4ff.

1 To understand political power right and derive it from its original, we must consider what state all men are naturally in, and 5 that is a state of perfect freedom to order their actions and dispose of their possessions and persons as they think fit, within the bounds of the law of nature, 10 without asking leave or depending upon the will of any other man. A state also of equality, wherein all the power and jurisdiction is reciprocal, no 15 one having more than another; there being nothing more evident than that creatures of the same species and rank [...] should also be equal one amongst another 20 without subordination or subjection. [...] The natural liberty of man is to be free from any superior power on earth, and not to be under the will or legislative authority of man, but to have only the law of nature for his rule. The liberty of man in 25 society is to be under no other legislative power but that established by consent in the commonwealth, nor under the dominion of any will or restraint of any law but what that legislative shall enact according to the trust put in it. If man in the state of nature be so free, [...] if he be 30 absolute lord of his own person and possessions, equal to the greatest and subject to nobody, why will he part with his freedom, why will he give up his empire and subject himself to the dominion and control of any other power? To which it is obvious to answer that though in 35 the state of nature he has such a right, yet the enjoyment of it is very uncertain and constantly exposed to the invasion of others. [...] This makes [man] willing to quit a condition which, however free, is full of fears and continual dangers; and [...] he seeks out and is willing 40 to join in society with others who are already united [...] for the mutual preservation of their lives, liberties, and estates, which I call by the general name of 'property'.

John Locke, 1632-1704

The great and chief end, therefore, of men's uniting into commonwealths and putting 45 themselves under government is the preservation of property. To which in the state of nature there are many things wanting: First, there wants an established, 50 settled, known law, received and allowed by common consent to be the standard of right and wrong. Secondly, in the state of nature there wants a known and 55 indifferent judge with authority to determine all differences according to the established law. Thirdly, in the state of nature there often wants power to back 60 and support the sentences when right, and to give it due execution. But though men when they enter into society give up the equality, liberty, and executive power they had in the state of nature into the hands of society, to be so far disposed 65 of by the legislative as the good of society shall require, the power of society, or legislative constituted by them, can never [...] extend farther than [...] to protect every one's property. [...]

The majority, having [...] the whole power of the 70 community naturally in them, may employ all that power in making laws for the community from time to time, and executing those laws by officers of their own appointing: and then the form of the government is a perfect democracy. The legislative or supreme authority cannot 75 assume to itself a power to rule by extemporary, arbitrary decrees, but is bound to dispense justice and to decide the rights of the subject by promulgated, standing laws, and known authorized judges. Though in a constituted commonwealth [...] there can be but one supreme power 80 which is the legislative, to which all the rest are and must be subordinate, yet, the legislative being only a fiduciary power to act for certain ends, there remains still in the people a supreme power to remove or alter

85 the legislative when they find the legislative act contrary to the trust reposed in them; whenever that end is manifestly neglected or opposed, the trust must necessarily be forfeited and the power devolve into the hands of those that gave it, who may place it anew where

90 they shall think best for their safety and security. The constitution of the legislative is the first and fundamental act of society, whereby provision is made for the continuation of their union under the direction of persons and bonds of laws made by persons authorized thereunto

95 by the consent and appointment of the people, without which no one man or number of men amongst them can have authority of making laws that shall be binding to the rest. When any one or more shall take upon them to make laws, whom the people have not appointed so to do, they make laws without authority, which the people 100 are not therefore bound to obey. To conclude, the power that every individual gave the society when he entered into it can never revert to the individuals again as long as the society lasts. But if they have set limits to the duration of their legislative and made this supreme power 105 in any person or assembly only temporary, or else when by miscarriage of those in authority it is forfeited, upon the forfeiture, or at the determination of the time set, it reverts to society and the people have a right to act as supreme and continue the legislative in themselves, or 110 erect a new form, or under the old form place it in new hands, as they think good.

Vocabulary

Title 1/treatise (n.): /'triːtiːz/ a serious book or article about a particular subject - **6 to order** (v.): to arrange s.th. according to a system or a plan - **6 to dispose** (of) (v.): to make use of - **9 bounds** (n., pl.): limit - **10 to ask leave**: to ask for the permission - **13 equality** (n.): a position in which people have the same rights - **14 jurisdiction** (n.): /ˌdʒʊərɪs'dɪkʃən ‖ ˌdʒʊr-/ the right to use an official power to make legal decisions - **14 reciprocal** (adj.): /rɪ'sɪprəkəl/ affecting each in the same way - **16 evident** (adj.): clear - **18 species** (n.): a group of animals or plants which are all similar and can breed - **18 rank** (n.): position within a group - **20 subordination** (n.): the act of putting o.s. or s.th. in a less important or inferior position - **11 subjection** (n.): the act of forcing s.o. to be ruled by another - **22 superior** (adj.): of higher rank or power - **23 legislative** (adj.): concerned with laws or making laws - **26 consent** (n.): permission or approval - **26 commonwealth** (n.): state - **27 dominion** (n.): highest authority - **27 restraint** (n.): here: a rule or principle that limits people's activity or behaviour - **28 to enact** (v.): to make into law - **29 be** (old subjunctive): is - **30 lord** (n.): here: master - **30 possessions** (n.,pl.): belongings - **31 subject** (adj.): /'sʌbdʒɪkt/ being under s.o.'s authority - **31 to part with** (v.): to give up, to abandon - **32 empire** (n.): large state - **33 to subject** (v.): /səb'dʒekt/ to force under the control of s.o. - **34 obvious** (adj.): clear - **35 enjoyment** (n.): the pleasure one gets from s.th. - **36 constantly** (adv.): all the time - **36 to expose** (to) (v.): to put s.o. in a position where they have no protection against danger - **37 invasion** (n.): the getting in by force - **37 to quit** (v.): to leave, to give up - **39 continual** (adj.): steadily coming back - **41 preservation** (n.): safekeeping - **42 estate** (n.): one's possessions - **43 chief** (adj.): main - **50 established** (adj.): recognized - **51 settled** (adj.): agreed on - **51 known** (adj.): known by many people - **51 received** (adj.): accepted to be correct - **52 allowed** (adj.): agreed that s.th. is permitted by the rules or the law - **56 indifferent** (adj.): showing neither interest nor dislike - **61 sentence** (n.): here: judgement (of a court) - **62 due** (adj.): proper or suitable - **65 to dispose (of)** (v.): to deal with s.th. such as a problem or a question successfully - **66 to require** (v.): to officially demand because there is a law or a rule - **67 to constitute** (v.): /'kɒnstɪtjuːt ‖ 'kɑːnstɪtuːt/ to establish - **68 to extend** (v.): to reach - **73 to execute** (v.): to carry out - **73 appointing** (n.): official choice - **75 supreme** (adj.): highest - **76 to assume** (v.): *here*: to give o.s. the right to - **76 extemporary** (adj.): not planned beforehand - **76 arbitrary** (adj.): /ɑː'rbɪtreri/ selected at one's will - **77 decree** (n.): official order - **77 to be bound to**: to be obliged to, to have to - **77 to dispense** (v.): to officially provide s.th. for people in a society - **78 to promulgate** (v.): to proclaim, to make known to the public - **78 standing** (adj.): permanently agreed or arranged - **79 authorized** (adj.): given official approval - **79 constituted** (adj.): established, with a constitution - **82 subordinate** (adj.): in a less important or inferior position - **83 fiduciary** (adj.): /fɪ'duːʃərɪ/ held in trust - **83 end** (n.): purpose, aim - **84 to remove** (v.): put away with - **84 to alter** (v.): to change, to modify - **85 contrary** (adj.): opposite in character, nature or position - **86 reposed** (adj.): placed - **87 manifest** (adj.): clear to the senses or to the mind - **87 to neglect** (v.): to leave unattended, not to pay attention to - **88 to forfeit** (v.): /'fɔːfɪt/ to lose the right by an error or a crime - **88 to devolve** (v.): to pass from one person to another - **89 anew** (adv.): over again - **92 provision** (n.): the act of giving s.th. which is necessary - **94 bonds** (n., pl.): s.th. that limits one's freedom and prevents people from doing what they want - **94 thereunto** (adv., arch.): to this - **97 binding** (adj.): having to be obeyed - **101 to conclude** (v.): to sum up at the end - **103 to revert** (v.): to return to (an original condition) - **105 duration** (n.): length of time - **106 temporary** (adj.): lasting for a short time only - **107 miscarriage** (n.): going wrong, being unsuccessful - **108 forfeiture** (n.): /'fɔːfɪtʃə/ loss of s.th. valuable as a punishment because of an error or a crime - **108 determination** (n.): decision - **108 set** (adj.): fixed - **111 to erect** (v.): to build, to bring into being

---

AWARENESS

1 When was the German Fundamental Law written? Find out as much as possible about its origins.
2 Why can the first nineteen articles of our constitution not be changed by any majority?
3 Study the American Constitution and try to find out if there are similar paragraphs in it that cannot be changed.

COMPREHENSION

4 What is the natural state like in which all human beings are by birth?
5 What is the only rule that everybody has to follow?
6 How far does the giving up of the freedom of humans only go?
7 Which right do the people always keep even if they have put the power into a legislative body?
8 How long does the power society has got from each individual last?

ANALYSIS

9 Make a list of the rights that Locke attributes to humans
   a) in the state of nature   b) in society.
10 Which ideas expressed in the American Declaration of Independence do you find in Locke's text?
    (You will find the text of the Declaration of Independence in the Resource Book.)

OPINION

11 Do you think any larger group of people who are dissatisfied with their government should have
    the right to found a state of their own? Give reasons.
12 If you had been in the place of the British King George III, would you have given the Americans the
    same rights as the British subjects? Give reasons for your decision.

PROJECTS

13 Find out more about the philosophical ideas about man and the state that prevailed during the Age
    of Enlightenment.
14 Make a list of what you expect your state to do for you and what you are willing to do for your state
    in return.

INTERNET PROJECTS

15 Study the German, the French, the American and the British constitutions and find out what they
    say about human rights. For detailed information, consult the following websites: www.lib.byu.edu/
    ~rdh/eurodocs/germ/ggeng.html ; http:xx en.wikipedia.org/wiki/French_Constitution_of_1791
    www.archives.gov/national_archives_experience/charters/declaration.html ; www.thinkhistory.
    btinternet.co.uk/britishconstitution.htm
16 Collect additional information on the Declaration of Independence and further American charters
    of freedom documents by using www.archives.gov/national_archives_experience/charters/
    declaration.html as a starting point.

2 | "WE THE PEOPLE OF THE UNITED STATES"

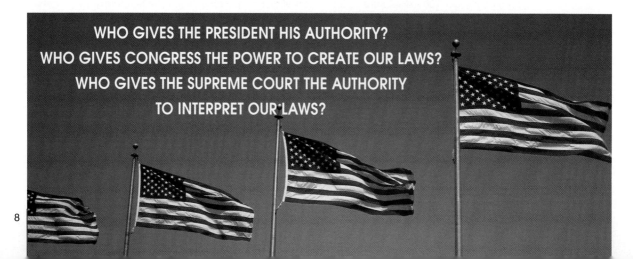

WHO GIVES THE PRESIDENT HIS AUTHORITY?
WHO GIVES CONGRESS THE POWER TO CREATE OUR LAWS?
WHO GIVES THE SUPREME COURT THE AUTHORITY
TO INTERPRET OUR LAWS?

"The Constitution does not solve
our problems.
It gives people freedom and
opportunity to solve their own
problems.
It gives representatives of the
people authority to help solve
problems.
It provides an executive to enforce
the laws and administer the
government.
It provides a judicial branch to say
what the law means.
From there on it is up to the
people."

*Warren E. Burger,
Chairman of the Commission, Chief
Justice of the United States (1969-1986)*

Supreme Court Justices

The U.S. Constitution – celebrating 200 years of successful government by the people.

Two hundred years ago, a document was drafted establishing the American system of government. No other people had ever written such a document. And the government it created has successfully endured longer than any of its kind in history.

In 1787, there was a need for a strong national government.

After the Continental Congress voted for independence from England in 1776, the "Articles of Confederation" were drafted, granting limited federal power. But the government could not levy taxes or regulate trade between the states or with foreign countries.

In America's early years, disputes often arose among the states. Locked into a clumsy structure, the U.S. government was too weak to enforce treaties or settle differences.

A decade after independence, it was apparent that the articles were ineffective. To survive, the national government needed a stronger foundation.

55 experienced delegates met to decide how the American government should function.

In May, 1787, the Constitutional Convention opened in Philadelphia. Its purpose was to strengthen the Articles of Confederation. But after some debate, it was agreed that a completely new government should be created.

The Convention delegates were a distinguished group comprised of some of the best educated, most respected men in the United States. They were men who had studied law, government, political theory, and history. Some of the delegates are familiar to you – George Washington, James Madison, Alexander Hamilton, and Benjamin Franklin.

The executive, legislative and judicial branches – a careful "separation of powers"

Many obstacles were faced and overcome during the course of the Convention. With some skilful compromise, a structure for the new government finally emerged.

There would be three equal branches of government. The Executive Branch, led by the President, who would administer the government.

The Legislative Branch, comprised of the Senate and the House of Representatives, would make the nation's laws.

And the Judicial Branch, consisting of our federal court judges, would interpret the laws for particular cases.

The Constitution grants power, limits power, and protects against abuses of power.

The Constitution assigned responsibilities and powers to each of these three branches and the government. At the same time, it provided for a system of "checks and balances" to ensure that no one branch could abuse its power.

To ratify or not to ratify – a long, hard struggle.

In September of 1787, the new Constitution was presented to the states for ratification. Supporters and opponents took up their positions, and a rich dialogue ensued which lasted for almost nine months.

The Federalists supported the Constitution. They believed a strong national government would help America prosper and compete with foreign countries. Since the government was responsible directly to America's citizens, they believed the rights of the people would be safe.

The Anti-Federalists felt differently. They argued that the Revolution had been fought to overcome excessive government power. They feared the new Constitution granted too much strength to the federal government, and would interfere with individual rights.

In the end, an addition – The Bill of Rights.

To guard against the loss of liberties, the first Congress agreed that a Bill of Rights should be added to the Constitution. The Bill of Rights, the first ten amendments, was ratified by the states and became part of the Constitution on December 15, 1791.

Amendments let the Constitution reflect change.

Through the years, other amendments have been added to the Constitution. There are now 26. The most recent was added in 1971, granting the vote to eighteen-year-olds.

Most of the amendments have either altered governmental structure or strengthened the Constitution's guarantee of equality and justice.

The ability to add amendments ensures the Constitution's vitality and effectiveness through changing times.

The basic principle – all political power rests with the people.

If there is one guiding principle of the U.S. Constitution, it is that power is granted to the government by those who are governed – We the people of the United States.

We the people are the foundation of our representative government.

Separation of Powers and Checks and Balances

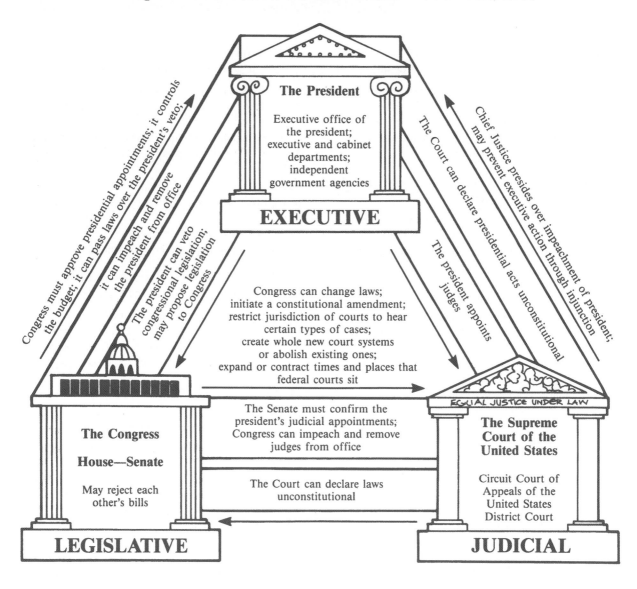

As Americans, we have rights and we have responsibilities.

Each person has the right to participate or not to participate in government.

However, an informed, involved citizenry is the best insurance for a continued free and representative government. Be involved in your community.

U.S. GOVERNMENT PRINTING OFFICE, The Constitution (Washington, D.C., 1990).

The Constitution is the foundation of the American way of life. Learn more about it.

Your public library is full of information on the history of the Constitution, the men who drafted it, and the functioning of the American government. To celebrate the birthday of the U.S. Constitution, learn about the illustrious document that has guaranteed our rights and kept the nation free for the past 200 years.

Vocabulary

9 executive (n.): s.o. who is part of a governing body - **9 to enforce** (v.): to apply - **10 to administer** (v.): to carry out - **21 to draft** (v.): to write down one's ideas - **24 to endure** (v.): to last - **30 to grant** (v.): to give - **31 to levy** (taxes) (v.): to demand or collect officially - **34 locked into** (adj.): - bound by; restricted by - **35 treaty** (n.): an agreement made between countries and formally signed by their representatives - **37 decade** (n.): ten years - **38 ineffective** (adj.): of no great use; of poor result - **46 distinguished** (adj.): /dɪˈstɪŋgwɪʃt/ outstandingly able; famous - **47 comprised** (adj.) (of): consisting of - **56 to emerge** (v.): to be the result of - **70 abuse** (n.): wrong or not authorized use - **67 to assign** (v.): to give to - **71 to ratify** (v.): to make a written agreement official by signing it - **75 to ensue** (v.): /ɪnˈsjuː ‖ ɪnˈsuː/ to be the consequence of - **78 to prosper** (v.): to become wealthy and powerful - **78 to compete** (v.): to measure one's forces with - **86 to interfere (with)** (v.): to enter into or take part in a matter in which one is not wanted - **90 amendment** (n.): an improvement made in or suggested for a rule, law, etc. - **98 to alter** (v.): to make or to become different - **101 to ensure** (v.): to make sure - **114 involved** (adj.): closely connected in relationship and activities with others - **114 citizenry** (n.) : /ˈsɪtɪzənri/ all the citizens of a state

Explanations

28 Continental Congress: the law-making body that governed the thirteen colonies that later formed the U.S. It passed the Declaration of Independence. - **42 Constitutional Convention**: (also Philadelphia Convention) the meeting of representatives in Philadelphia in 1787 that led to the writing of the Constitution of the U.S.A. - **43 Articles of Confederation**: the agreement drawn up in 1781 by the 13 original colonies of the U.S. which served as the basic law for the government until the U.S. Constitution was agreed upon in 1788 - **50 George Washington** (1732-1799): commander in chief of the army of the thirteen colonies, after the War of Independence first President of the United States (1789-97) - **51 James Madison** (1751-1836): 4th President of the U.S. (1809-17) and leading statesman during the War of Independence, one of the authors of the Declaration of Independence - **51 Alexander Hamilton** (1757-1804): leading federalist and main advocate of the Constitution of 1787 - **51 Benjamin Franklin** (1706-1790): diplomat and inventor (Franklin-stove, a new kind of clock, lightning rod), was ambassador in France, negotiated with England and became the first secretary of state (=foreign minister) under President George Washington - **76 Federalist**: a member of a political party (founded in 1787) which was in favor of a strong federal government

AWARENESS

1 Working in groups, gather information about the German Constitution (Fundamental Law). As a useful Internet source you can use www.datenschutz-berlin.de/recht/de/gg/.
   a) When was it drafted and why?
   b) Who were the authors?

COMPREHENSION

2 Why did 55 experienced delegates meet in Philadelphia in May 1787?
3 What was the main structure of the new Constitution of September 1787?
4 What does the term "checks and balances" mean?
5 How can the American Constitution be modernized to react to changes in society?
6 What was the first major modification of the new Constitution and why had it become necessary?

INTERNET PROJECT

7 Working in groups, find out major similarities and differences between the American and German constitutions:
   a) the U.S. Senate and the Bundesrat   b) the U.S. House of Representatives and the Bundestag
   c) the U.S. President and the Bundespräsident d) the U.S. Government and the Bundesregierung
   As starting points, use the following internet sources:
   http:xx thomas.loc.gov/home/legbranch/ legbranch.html ; http:xx bensguide.gpo.gov/9-12/index.html;
   http://de.wikipedia.org./wiki/wahlrecht ; www.bundesregierung.de/ ; www.bundestag.de/htdocs e/
   index.html .

Peter Vilbig & Stacey Delikat

3 "enough is ENOUGH"

Americans get millions of unsolicited phone calls and junk e-mails. Congress is acting to limit them. But marketers say they have a free-speech right to make their pitches. - Peter Vilbig & Stacey Delikat, "enough is Enough", *The New York Times UPFRONT* (September 22, 2003), pp.12-15.

IF THE INTERNET WERE REALLY AN INFORMATION SUPERHIGHWAY -

ENTER

In Washington, D.C., 18-year-old Harry Stein had his aha! moment on Internet spam - the unsolicited junk e-mail that clogs millions of in-boxes across America - when the family returned from a weeklong vacation. The Stein e-mail account was buried in over 100 e-mail messages, the vast majority of them spam.

"It took almost an hour and a half to go through it," says Stein, who is starting his freshman year at the University of Wisconsin this fall. "We were taking turns deleting it. One of us would come in and do 30, and then another would do another 50." The family quickly bought a service that helps filter Internet spam from their e-mail accounts.

Halfway across the U.S. in St. Louis, Nikki Elwood, 16, says Internet spam is an annoyance, but even more frustrating are the calls from telemarketers bombarding her house with sales pitches. The calls come throughout the day and even into the night. [...] "We've gotten to where we just hang up."

50 Percent and Growing

Modern communications in the form of the phone and the Internet have turned what were once the infrequent knocks of traveling salespeople on the doors of American homes into daily home invasions. Telemarketers make about 65 million phone calls a day, and the spam onslaught is worse: By the end of 2003, 7.1 trillion spam messages will have been sent, according to Brightmail, a spam detection company. That's up from 3.6 trillion in 2002. By last July, 50 percent of e-mail was spam.

The constant assault has put the U.S. Congress in the position of refereeing a classic battle between voters angry at the sales pitches and marketers who stand to lose billions if their entryway into American homes is slammed shut. For years marketing groups used lobbying clout to stall congressional bills aimed at their operations. But the mood in Congress shifted this year - some say because members themselves are fed up with the hard sell. Congress limited telemarketing calls in a bill President George W. Bush signed into law in June. The bill created a national do-not-call list. This fall, the House of Representatives and the Senate are expected to take up legislation aimed at spam.

Invasion of Privacy or Free Speech?

"We have to deal with the problem," says U.S. Senator Conrad Burns, Republican of Montana, a sponsor of one version of the antispam legislation before Congress. "Doing nothing is not an option."

But the outcome of the battle over unsolicited marketing is far from certain. Groups representing the $100-billion-a-year telemarketing industry have already gone to court challenging the new antitelemarketing law. They argue that it restricts their right to freedom of speech under the Constitution's First Amendment. Because the telemarketing law allows political fundraising calls, telemarketers also say it violates the 14th Amendment's equal protection clause, which holds that laws must be applied in the same way for everyone.

But millions of Americans see the marketing calls as a violation of what they hold to be a basic right to privacy - in other words, the right to be left alone. The privacy right isn't guaranteed in a specific amendment, but in the landmark 1965 case Griswold v. Connecticut, the Supreme Court ruled that the Fourth Amendment, which bans illegal searches and seizures, along with several other amendments, implies such a right.

The nation's new telemarketing law was an immediate hit. In its first three weeks of registering phone numbers, nearly 30 million people signed up for the list by calling a 1-800 number or visiting a government Website (www.donotcall.gov). Federal officials say they expect 60 million people will register by next summer. Beginning October 1, telemarketers could be heavily fined for calling numbers on the list.

An Uphill Battle?

But while grateful for the new law, opponents of telemarketing say the legislation was watered down under industry pressure and may be ineffective.

80 "There are so many loopholes you can drive a boiler room through it," says Robert V. Arkow, president of Californians Against Telephone Solicitation. (Boiler room is the slang term used to describe shady telemarketing operations that are sometimes run out of
85 basements.) The new law, for instance, allows telemarketers within a state to keep making calls, unless that state's own laws forbid them.

Loopholes could become a problem in the antispam legislation the Congress will likely consider this fall.
90 Opponents have already targeted a bill proposed by two powerful Republicans, Billy Tauzin of Louisiana, chairman of the Energy and Commerce Committee, and F. James Sensenbrenner Jr. of Wisconsin, chairman of the Judiciary Committee. Their bill would normally be
95 a frontrunner. In order to push favored bills through, committee chairs can use their powers to determine when legislation is scheduled for hearings and votes.

But opponents of the antispam bill say lobbyists from the credit card industry and other factions have used
100 their influence with lawmakers to make certain the new law only outlaws marketing e-mail whose "primary purpose" is to promote a product. By pretending that selling is only the secondary purpose of their e-mails, marketers could skirt the law, opponents of the bill say.

Finding the Loopholes

Major Internet service providers have sued spammers trying to stop the flood of messages, and spent millions of dollars on software that attempts to filter out spam.

Yet the flood of spam shows little sign of abating, with the number of messages doubling in the last year. 110 Ferris Research, a communications consulting company, estimates the cost of spam in lost time for workers and business spending at $10 billion a year. If spam keeps growing, some fear it could make e-mail unworkable as a communications tool. 115

Most spammers hide their identities and don't come forward to defend their practices. But one e-mail marketer, who says she runs a legitimate business that helps people with bad credit, says spam is getting a bad rap. With e-mail, she says she reaches millions of people 120 who benefit from her expertise.

"These antispammers should get a life," says Alyx Sachs, a California-based marketer. "Do their fingers hurt too much from pressing the delete key? How much time does that really take from their day?" 125

But many computer users say spam is more than a minor inconvenience. "Every single day, two or three times a day, I'm erasing multiple messages that I have to spend at least a few seconds glancing at to make sure it's not something I need," says Brian Basham, a real- 130 estate broker in downtown Denver. "By the end of the year, who knows how many hours I spent looking at this stupid stuff to figure out what's junk?"

Vocabulary

Intro 1/unsolicited (adj.): not asked for and often not wanted - **Intro 1/junk** (n.): old or unwanted objects that have no use or value - **Intro 2/marketer** (n.): /ˈmɑːkɪtə ‖ mɑːrkɪtər/ s.o. who sells goods or services - **Intro 2/to make a pitch** (for s.th.) (v.): to try to persuade people to do s.th. - **2 spam** (n.): e-mail messages that a computer user has not asked for and does not want to read, for example, from s.o. who is advertising s.th. - **3 to clog** (v.): to block s.th. or become blocked - **3 inbox** (n.): the place in a computer e-mail program where new messages arrive - **8 freshman** (n.): (AmE) student in the first year of high school or university - **10 to delete** (v.): to remove s.th. that has been written down or stored in a computer - **19 to hang up** (v.): *here:* to finish a telephone conversation - **22 infrequent** (adj.): not happening often - **26 onslaught** (n.): a violent attack - **30 assault** (n.): /əˈsɔːlt ‖ əˈsɒːlt/ violent attack - **31 to referee** (v.): to make sure that the rules are followed - **34 to slam shut** (v.): to close with a loud noise - **35 to lobby** (v.): to try to persuade the government or someone with political power that a law or situation should be changed - **36 clout** (n.): power or the authority to influence other people's decisions - **36 to stall** (v.): to stop making progress or developing - **37 to shift** (v.): to change a situation, discussion, etc., by giving special attention to one idea or subject

instead of to a previous one - **53 to challenge** (v.): to question the rightness, legality, etc. of - **57 fundraising** (n.): the activity of collecting money for a specific purpose, esp. in order to help people who are ill, old, etc. - **64 landmark** (n.): one of the most important events, changes, or discoveries that influences s.o. or s.th. - **66 seizure** (n.): /ˈsiːʒə ‖ -ər/ when police or government officers take s.th. away from s.o. - **69 to register** (v.): to put s.o.'s name on an official list - **75 to fine** (v.): to make s.o. pay money as a punishment - **80 loophole** (n.): a small mistake in a law that makes it possible to avoid doing s.th. that the law is supposed to make you do - **95 frontrunner** (n.): the person or thing that is most likely to succeed in a competition - **96 chair** (n.): *here:* the person who is in charge of a committee - **104 to skirt** (v.): *here:* to avoid talking about an important subject - **106 to sue** (v.): to make a legal claim against s.o., esp. for money because they have harmed you in some way - **109 to abate** (v.): to become less strong or decrease - **119 bad rap** (n.): (AmE informal) unfair treatment or punishment - **122 get a life** (spoken): used to tell s.o. you think they are boring - **128 to erase** (v.): *here:* to remove information from a computer memory - **130 real estate** (n.): property in the form of land or houses - **131 broker** (n.): s.o. who arranges sales or business agreements for other people

Explanations

Intro/Congress: the law-making body of the U.S. consisting of the Senate and the House of Representatives. Congress decides whether a bill (= a suggested law) becomes a law. If the Senate and the House of Representatives both agree to a bill, the President is asked to agree. The President can say no to the bill (veto), but Congress can still make it a law if two-thirds of the members of each house agree. - **42**
House of Representatives: the larger and more powerful of the two parts of the central law-making organization in the U.S. The House has 435 members, called Representatives or Congressmen/women, elected by their state. The number of Representatives per state depends on the size of its population. A Representative serves for two years. - **43**
Senate: the smaller of the two parts of the central law-making body in the U.S. The U.S. Senate has 100 senators, two from each state, who are elected by the people in that state. A senator serves for six years. - **55 Constitution**: the highest law of the government of the U.S., consisting of seven articles and 25* amendments (= a change to the original) which were written down in 1787 and officially came into use in 1789. The Constitution of the U.S. sets out how the government should be formed and what the right of States and individuals are. When it was first written, the rights of individuals were not included, but in 1791 ten Amendments (additions) known as the Bill of Rights were added. Most Americans would recognize the Preamble (beginning statement) of the Constitution, which reads, "We the people of the United States, in order to form a more perfect union, establish justice, insure domestic tranquility, provide for the common defense, promote the general welfare, and secure the blessings of liberty to ourselves and our posterity, to ordain and establish this Constitution for the United States of America." - **55 First Amendment**: a part of the American Constitution which gives American citizens the rights of freedom of speech, freedom of the press, and freedom of assembly (= the right to gather together as a group). Many cases concerning the rights included in the First Amendment have been taken to the Supreme Court. People in the U.S. usually feel very strongly about the questions that these cases raise. - **65 Supreme Court**: the highest court and final court of appeal in the U.S. federal system. The U.S. Supreme Court has nine judges, called justices, who are on the court as long as they wish to serve. The president suggests suitable judges for the court when a position becomes open, and the Senate must approve of his choice. The Supreme Court decides which cases it wants to hear, and these cases often attract a lot of public attention. Cases which come before the Supreme Court often concern the U.S. Constitution, such as the right to free speech.
From: *Longman Dictionary of English Language and Culture* (Longman Group Ltd., Harlow, 1992)

*) At present, there are 27 amendments.

AWARENESS

1 Have you ever been bothered by unsolicited phone calls and junk e-mails? Have you heard of other people's experiences with Internet spam and telemarketers who solicit business over the phone?

COMPREHENSION

2 Why was Harry Stein so annoyed when looking at his e-mail account after he had returned from a week-long vacation?
3 Why does Nikki Elwood find telemarketing even more frustrating than Internet spam?
4 What are the economic implications if spam keeps growing?
5 In what way are the regulation of telemarketing and the antispam legislation made ineffective according to critics?

CARTOON ANALYSIS

6 The cartoons (p. 12 and p. 18) deal with the Internet as an information superhighway and the impact of spam on using the Internet. What messages do these cartoons convey?

OPINION

7 As a computer user, do you consider Internet spam a major annoyance or a minor inconvenience? Give examples to support your decision.
8 Do you think that unsolicited marketing is an invasion of privacy and should be banned or do you support the argument that antitelemarketing laws restrict the right to freedom of speech?
9 The right to privacy and the right to free speech are highly important values in a democratic society. Are they of equal importance or can one be given priority over the other?

INTERNET PROJECT

10 Find out if in the European Union or in Germany any antitelemarketing laws and antispam legislation ban or limit unsolicited phone calls and junk e-mails. As a starting point, you might find the following website useful for your research: www.teltarif.de/i/spam-recht.html.

Peter Bromhead

"The Parties"

Compared to European democracies, the American party system seems simple and easy to grasp: either you vote Republican or you vote Democrat. Even odd birds like Ross Perot, who was the third can-didate for presidency in 1992 and 1996, have not been able to change the picture of the American party system. Perot had his supporters, but he did not found a new party. If you take a closer look behind the scenes or study the history of the two major parties, however, you will find astounding facts that are likely to topple the impression that for Americans the decision at an election, whether state or national, is easy and clear-cut. - Peter Bromhead, *Life in Modern America* (Burnt Mill, Harlow: Longman Group, 1988), pp. 64-67.

1 It has been said that the two great American parties are like two bottles, both empty, one labelled 'Re-publican', the other 'Democrat'. And 5 if the two bottles do have anything in them, some ingredients change continuously from one to the other; so any attempt to describe either party needs endless and complex 10 qualification. Around 1850 the two parties were the Whigs and the Democrats. The old Democrats tended to support state autonomy against the central government. In 1854 15 a northern alliance of people determined to abolish slavery founded a new party, which they called 'Republican' (reviving an old name). It rapidly absorbed the Whigs. Abraham Lincoln was the first Republican President in 1861-65, and the Republicans were 20 identified with the northern fight in the Civil War for a Union free of slavery. Afterwards they represented the main stream of developing northern industry and free private enterprise. Outside the South the Democrats attracted the support of the groups who felt themselves 25 to be outside the dominant system: around 1900 the less favoured immigrants from Eastern Europe and Ireland, and as time went on other non-insiders too, whether poor or Jewish or intellectuals or Catholic or (very much later) blacks. As labour unions grew up, most of them 30 supported the Democrats. Since 1933 the Democrats have been the party of the left - outside the South. The 1932 election was fought in the midst of the worst economic depression ever experienced. Probably a quarter of the people were unemployed, without any 35 systematic relief. Franklin D. Roosevelt won, and led his Democrats with his 'New Deal' programme, involving federal and state intervention in the economy and the beginnings of governmental social services. In the next forty years the Democrats pushed these policies further, 40 particularly during the presidencies of Kennedy and Johnson. Since the beginning of the seventies there has been little real progress in this direction. The Republicans have, at least since 1900, shown more qualities associated

At a Republican Party convention

with the right: less government intervention in the economy; little 45 enthusiasm for new social programmes; patriotic language (but in practice until 1980 a cautious foreign policy); much talk about the responsibility of the individual, and 50 about state and local autonomy. They are in general supported by business interests. Southern politics are different. Because of its origin, the Republican party could gain no 55 support at all among the dominant southern white population. For many decades there was only one party in the South, the Democrats. All political contests were contests between factions of the Democratic party – and the most 60 conservative factions usually won. So in the U.S. Senate and House of Representatives the southern states were represented always by Democrats, often more conservative than any Republican from the North. By the 1960s many conservative southerners transferred their 65 allegiance to the Republicans. Since then all the southern states have elected some Republicans as governors and to the U.S. Congress, and have supported some Republicans for the U.S. Presidency - Ronald Reagan in particular. Meanwhile, with the blacks and other 70 minorities in the South taking a full part in politics, they in their turn support the Democrats. In parts of the South the old Democratic party still dominates local politics, with right and left (and other) factions contesting primary elections within the party, while in national politics there 75 is serious rivalry between the Democrats and Republicans, as in most other areas of the nation. Meanwhile the main, or 'liberal' body of the Democratic Party now has its most solid basis in the northern cities, and particularly among trade union members and among 80 the black and other ethnic inner-city groups. But these cities do not dominate their states in terms of population. There are more people in the suburbs than in the central cities. To win a majority in the House of Representatives the Democrats need to attract votes on a wide basis. In 85 fact, all through the 1970s and 1980s, with Republicans

A supporter of the Democratic Party

as Presidents for sixteen years out of twenty, the Democrats had big majorities in the House of Representatives, controlled most state legislatures, and held the governorships of most states (sometimes two-thirds or more). They lost the Senate only in the first six years of Reagan's presidency, and in 1986 regained the majority there that they had enjoyed throughout the 1970s. Such widespread electoral success could not be achieved by a party which Europeans would regard as a party of the left. Although the left is contained within the Democratic Party, the party as a whole is based on interests so diverse and scattered that it cannot easily have a coherent party policy. Some of the people elected as Democrats to state and national offices could be considered as being, on the left/right scale, more to the right than their Republican opponents.

Within some states there are some cities, or other areas with substantial populations, where one of the two parties (usually the Democrats) has a virtual monopoly of power and electoral support. In such places the dominant party's candidates are sure to win, and the real electoral contest is at the dominant party's primary election between rival factions based on ethnic or material interests. Both in these one-party areas and elsewhere there are often five or six rivals for a party's nomination at a primary, and many states provide for a 'run-off' (second ballot) a week or more later, between the two candidates who had most votes at the first. The Republicans have always been linked with business large and small, and with the idea that free enterprise is at the foundation of the nation's character. After the disasters of Watergate and the 1976 election, the Republican National Committee began a vigorous campaign to build up a well-funded central party organisation through which a coherent party policy might be developed, capable of translating a clear conservative philosophy into ideas of action. The Reagan presidency has not had much success in its pursuit of sound national finance, or in its aim of reducing federal intervention in the social welfare budget, but it has effectively identified the Republican party with the moral and patriotic feelings of the 'silent majority' of the people - though obviously some members of this majority have voted for Democrats for some offices.

Vocabulary

Intro 1/to grasp (v.): to understand - **Intro 4/to found** (v.): to begin the development of - **Intro 5/astounding** (adj.): astonishing; surprising - **Intro 5/to topple** (v.): to upset; to overthrow - **3 to label** (v.): to stick a small piece of paper on an object to indicate its contents or character - **6 ingredient** (n.): a particular one of a mixture of things, esp. in baking - **10 qualification** (n.): *here:* explanation of the different aspects - **15 alliance** (n.): a close connection between countries - **17 to revive** (v.): to call back to life - **17 to absorb** (v.): to suck up or take in like a sponge - **23 enterprise** (n.): an organization, esp. a business firm - **27 non-insider** (n.): s.b. who is not really integrated - **29 labour union** (n.): organization that defends the rights of the workers - **33 depression** (n.): a period of reduced business activity and of high unemployment - **35 relief** (n.): the feeling of comfort at the end of a period of fear - **36 to involve** (v.): to make s.o. mixed in s.th. - **39 policy** (n.): a plan or course of action - **43 associated with** (v.): connected with - **48 cautious** (adj.): /ˈkɔːʃəs/ careful - **55 to gain** (v.): to win - **59 contest** (n.): a struggle or fight in which two or more people compete for victory - **60 faction** (n.): the part of a larger group with well-defined ideas - **66 allegiance** (n.): loyalty; support - **73 to dominate** (v.): to rule over s.o. because one is stronger - **81 ethnic** (adj.): related to a racial, national or tribal group - **93 legislature** (n.): /ˈledʒɪsleɪtʃə/ the law-making body in a democracy - **94 governorship** (n.): the post of a governor - **104 electoral (**adj.): connected with an election - **109 to scatter** (v.): to spread about irregularly - **110 coherent** (adj.): able to stick together; forming a logical entity - **113 scale** (n.): the standard of estimation or

judgement - **116 virtual** (adj.): being almost the same - **122 nomination** (n.): proposal or choice of a candidate - **123 ballot** (n.): system of voting - **128 disaster** (n.): a catastrophe - **130 vigorous** (adj.): strong; intense - **130 well-funded** (adj.): with more than enough money - **134 pursuit** (n.): /pərˈsjuːt ‖ pərˈsuːt/ the act of following s.th. or looking for s.th. - **136 budget** (n.): the sum of money one plans to get and to spend

Explanations

Intro 2/ Henry Ross Perot: (*1930) a wealthy American who entered the 1992 and 1996 presidential elections and enjoyed a lot of popular support, even though he was not connected with either of the main political parties. Voters thought he was more honest and direct than other politicians. - **11 Whigs**: originally (ca. 1834-1855) the American Liberals who wanted to strengthen the individual rights against the state. They represented propertied and professional interests. - **18 Abraham Lincoln**: (1809-1865) 16th president of the U.S., led the North against the South. - **20 Civil War**: the war between the American South and the North (1861-1865), which began when 11 southern states rebelled against the U.S. Federal government. The war was caused mainly by the disagreement over slavery. The South wanted to keep slavery because of the huge plantations, the North wanted to have slavery abolished all over the United States. The North won, and the South took a long and difficult time to recover from the collapse of its economy. - **35 Franklin D. Roosevelt**: (1882-1945) the 32nd president of the U.S., serving from 1933-1945. He was president during the Great Depression and was responsible for his country's efforts during World War II, during which he was elected for the third and fourth times. - **40 John Fitzgerald Kennedy (JFK)**: (1917-1963) the 35th president of the U.S. (1961-1963), a Democrat and the first Roman Catholic to be elected. He was shot and killed in Dallas, Texas. JFK is remembered because of the Bay of Pigs Invasion of Cuba in 1961 and his program of social change which was carried out by Lyndon Johnson after Kennedy's death. Kennedy was very popular and people were sad when he was killed, although since that time many facts have appeared showing that his character and behavior were not as good as they seemed. **41 Lyndon Baines Johnson**: (1908-1973) the 36th president of the U.S. (1963-69), a Democrat. As John F. Kennedy's vice-president, Johnson became president when Kennedy was killed. He was re-elected in 1964 and helped start many social programs in his plans for a Great Society, but he became unpopular after increasing U.S. involvement in Vietnam. - **69 Ronald Wilson Reagan**: (1911-2004) an American Republican politician, who was the 40th president of the U.S. (1981-1989). He is also known for having been a film actor before he became a politician. - **128 Watergate**: a building complex in Washington, D.C., where the Democrats had their election campaign headquarters for the Congress elections of 1975. The then president Nixon was involved in the attempt to break into the headquarters to find out what the Democrats were planning. Reporters of the Washington Post found out about Nixon's involvement, so the President left office before Congress could dismiss ("impeach") him. For a long time, the Republicans were discredited and lost the next presidential election in 1976.

AWARENESS

1 Which political parties are represented in
   a) your regional parliament,   b) your national parliament?
2 Where do these parties stand with regard to the traditional left-wing and right-wing classification in politics?
3 Do the major parties have factions? If so, give examples.

COMPREHENSION

4 What do some humorous people compare the two great American parties to?
5 Why is it so difficult to describe the two major parties?
6 Why can the Democrats be called a party of the left outside the South after 1933?
7 What have the Republicans been associated with since 1900?
8 Why can the Democratic Party not be called a leftist party like the European socialists or social democrats?
9 What has always been a main electoral source for the Republicans?

ANALYSIS

10 Divide the text into paragraphs and find subtitles for each of your paragraphs.
11 Make a list of the main characteristics of the Democrats and the Republicans.
12 Find out when there were major changes in the development of the parties and their electorates. Look for explanations outside the text: what were the major political events in the United States when these changes happened?

OPINION

13 What do you think about having only two rivaling parties which in themselves have many diverse factions?
14 What is your opinion about the fact that in the U.S. there can be a president of one party, and the majority of the other party dominates the House of Representatives and/or the Senate?
15 After having studied the text carefully, do you think a president would have an easy life if both Houses were dominated by his party? Give examples and use arguments to support your decision.

PROJECTS

16 When you analyze the policies of German parties, which aspects would be likely to figure in the programs of the Republicans and the Democrats?
17 Study the interview with Dudley Buffa (text no. 5, pages 18f.) and decide which of the two parties is most likely to appeal to the "new constituency", the knowledge workers. Give reasons.

INTERNET PROJECT

18 In the illustrations inserted in the text about the American parties, the elephant and the donkey are associated as emblems or party mascots with the Republicans and the Democrats.
Find out about the origin of these symbolic figures and collect more examples of specific cartoons. Use the following Internet source as a starting point for your research: www.politicalcartoons.com/.

5

Dudley Buffa

"The Future of American Democracy"*

The American electoral system has become so complicated in the course of time that on the average only 50% of those who have the right to vote actually participate in the elections. Within the parties the process of choosing the right candidates is equally complicated and costs a lot of money, time and energy. It is not surprising, then, that in a changing world people think that certain "rituals" should change, too. When you think of today's possibilities in the fields of media and electronic communication, it seems evident into what direction a reform will go. - Dudley Buffa, "The Future of American Democracy"* (San Francisco: Interview by Gerti Schön, German translation published in: *Frankfurter Rundschau*, 30 September 1996), p.10.

1   **Frankfurter Rundschau (FR):** How do you want to change the election process, a mode of election to a more - kind of - basic democracy?

Buffa: That is a very good question. It is perhaps less
5 a question of how we would like to change it than the way in which the technology is taking it. There is a certain logic to the technology. You have been witnessing, like the rest of us, what may turn out to be the last two major political party conventions as we know them in
10 this country. There are both the Republican Convention and the Democratic Convention that have been dismissed in many quarters as simply very expensive "infomercials". It's tough to quarrel with that judgement. Television has changed American politics. Television has put a premium
15 on candidates or political parties that are able to generate large amounts of money so that they can buy the very expensive television time they need to get their message or even their names across to the public. The internet and the kind of computers that are connected to the internet
20 will begin to change this. It will begin to change this in that it is virtually free to put a message out on the internet. Moreover, as people become used to the computer the same way that an older generation was used to writing things with pencil and paper, they would be able to find
25 the information they want; they will have less interest in watching television commercials in which one side beats up on the other and be far more interested in getting the kind of hard facts they want, on the basis of which they can make an informed decision. We believe, and in
30 the book "Taking Control" we argue, that you go and see an end to the present arrangement by which we elect the President of the
35 United States. Then which we are going to see in its place, is a system in which some parties may wish to meet in a convention but
40 if they do, it will be to nominate candidates to run in a nation-wide primary.

There will be one primary in which some candidates will be nominated simply by achieving a certain level of support as indicated by those that in effect sign an
45 electronic petition by using a secured signature on the internet to register their support for candidate X or candidate Y. Once they have reached whatever the threshold is, then they become qualified to run in this national primary. The two top vote-getters, and it would
50 be a popular vote, would then run off against each other in the same way we now have the election in November. But anyway, you are going to see the continued decline of popular support for major political parties. I think you will see the emergence of new political parties. And
55 the dominant political force in this country is going to be that first politician or party that fashions an appeal to this new constituency that we think will be the dominant constituency in the 21st century, these knowledge workers.
60

FR: How can they affect politics, and you were talking about a new contract right now; will they have the power to influence the whole way of making politics as much that the politics are changing?

Buffa: Oh, I think that is probably true. The interesting
65 thing that we have just finished at the Institute for the New California is the first poll that has ever been taken by which to try to establish the actual number of knowledge workers in California and what their political attitudes and general points of view are. Politicians who
70 always want to attract majority support will start trying to appeal to this group. This group in turn, through that required appeal, will change the way politicians
75 talk about politics. These knowledge workers in combination with the technology will change the way we do politics in this
80 country.

FR: What kind of values, what attitudes do most knowledge workers have?

85 **Buffa**: It will sound a little glib, but actually knowledge workers turn out to be simply smart; they do not buy into this notion that Democrats just want to have big government 90 for the sake of big government, and they do not buy into the other notion of Republicans, you know, just want to do whatever they have to do, to reduce taxes maybe and eliminate 95 government. They do not buy into either the caricatures one party makes of the other, nor do they buy into the more general proposition that you have to choose, for example, between having effective government and having a government you can afford. They have learned 100 that by using the technology they are able to do a lot more things with a lot less effort. They have seen that the technology has improved almost everything without raising the price. So they want more for less.

FR: Is it time for a new party?

105 **Buffa**: I think it is probably time for a new party. Now let me be careful about something: you could end up, and it has happened before in American history, where one of the existing major parties undergoes the kind of transformation so that while it continues to have the 110 name it had before, it really stands for something altogether different. If neither one of the two major

parties responds to this new constituency and responds to the requirements of the information age, I think there is no question that 115 you will have a third party that does. The existence of what is already 25% of the workforce with clearly identifiable common opinions, common points of view, common 120 interests, won't simply sit there with nobody trying to fashion a message to appeal to them. And if the two parties remain too close to their own extremes, in other words, if the Republicans stay too locked-in with the Evangelical Christians that make up 125 the right wing of that party, if the Democrats, on the other hand, remain too locked-in to, for example, the teachers' unions and some of the industrial unions that dominate its old base, if that happens, then you will see the continued decline in support of both of them. Right 130 now 62% of the American people are favorably disposed toward the possibility of a third party. There are more people now in this country who call themselves independents than identify themselves with either the Democrats or Republicans. If that does not change, then 135 yes, absolutely, there will be a third party, and that third party will most certainly be designed to appeal to this new constituency.

Vocabulary

2 mode (n.): way, method - **7 to witness** (v.): to be present at the time when s.th. happens - **9 major** (adj.): here: big; important - **9 party convention** (n.): meeting of all the members or delegates of a political party - **11 to dismiss** (v.): (to send away); here: to put out of one's mind - **12 infomercials** (n.): information and commercials, i.e. the presentation of information as in advertising - **13 tough** (adj.): /tʌf/ hard - **14 premium** (n.): high value; extra price - **15 to generate** (v.): to collect; to get - **17 to get s.th. across**: to make s.th. clear to s.o. - **21 virtual** (adj.): /'vɔːtʃuəl ‖ 'vɜːr-/ practical - **27 to beat (up on)** (v.): to attack with words or arguments that are not necessarily true - **33 arrangement** (n.): mode or way - **41 to run** (v.): to be a candidate in an election process - **45 to indicate** (v.): to point out or suggest - **46 petition** (n.): a formal written demand - **46 secured** (adj.): made safe - **49 threshold** (n.): /'θreʃhəʊld/ here: lowest level which must be reached - **51 to run off against**: to be the official opponent of s.o. - **53 decline** (n.): a change to a lower state or level - **55 emergence** (n.): coming up; appearance - **56 dominant** (adj.): main; most important - **57 to fashion** (v.): to form; to work out - **57 appeal** (n.): attractiveness - **58 constituency** (n.): in a democracy the number of persons within a district who can vote for one or more representatives in parliament - **61 to affect** (v.): to influence - **67 poll** (n.): a questioning of a number of people chosen by chance to find out the general opinion about s.th. or s.o. - **69 to establish** (v.): to find out or make certain - **73 in turn**: as a reaction - **74 to require** (v.): to need; to expect - **82 value** (n.): /'væljuː/ guiding principle or idea - **85 glib** (adj.): spoken too easily to be true - **88 to buy into** (v.): to believe; to accept - **90**

for the sake of: for the reason or purpose of - **91 notion** (n.): idea; opinion - **94 to eliminate** (v.): to get rid of - **95 caricature** (n.): /'kærɪkətʃuə/ distorted picture by exaggerating the negative or funny sides - **97 proposition** (n.): s.th. that is proposed to a person for consideration - **99 to afford** (v.): to be able to buy or pay for - **112 to respond** (v.): to answer; to react - **114 requirement** (n.): /rɪ'kwaɪəmənt/ need; demand - **118 workforce** (n.): all the people who work in factories and in industry generally - **119 identifiable** (adj.): /aɪ'dentɪfaɪəbl/ which can be recognized - **125 locked-in** (adj.): closely connected - **128 union** (n.): here: trade union - **131 favourably disposed**: approving - **137 designed** (adj.): planned; organized

Explanations

30 *Taking Control*: a book by Dudley Buffa and others about the latest development of technology and how technology will influence everyday life in California - **42 primary** (n.): election among party members and sympathizers to choose their candidate for the presidency - **60 knowledge worker** (n.): a word coined by Dudley Buffa and his colleagues for s.b. "who uses a computer at his work; this computer is tied in with other computers as a network on the job." - **66 Institute for a New California**: a research institute, part of Berkeley University, dealing with new ways and manners for the technological development of California - **125 Evangelical Christians**: a collective name for several groups within the orthodox Protestant Christian church whose views and attitudes (particularly to religious ceremonies) often vary.

1 In which fields of everyday life do computers play an important role today? Make a list.
2 Which of the above-listed possibilities have you already used?
3 How were things done before people had computers?

COMPREHENSION

4 Why does D. Buffa think that today's technology will change the election process without the interference of man?
5 How will computers change the major political parties' traditional way of making their presidential candidate known to a wider public?
6 What does D. Buffa think about the future of the two major political parties in the United States?
7 Why will the knowledge workers change the way politics are conducted in the U.S.?
8 What might happen to the existing two major parties if they do not change their policies?

ANALYSIS

9 Make a list of the changes that modern technology may bring about in the election process.
10 Find out what changes the American party system will have to undergo to become attractive to the "new constituency", the knowledge workers.
11 Compare the changes that modern technology may bring about with the changes that knowledge workers will demand. Show how both are connected.

OPINION

12 Do you think D. Buffa is right when he says that the use of computers at school and in jobs will form a new generation of people? Give reasons.
13 Do you think that your parents' and grandparents' generations will adapt to the information age? Discuss in this context the message of the cartoon.
14 Do you think the knowledge workers might vote for a party that corresponds to the Greens? Why/why not?

PROJECT

15 Work out a set of slogans for an election campaign appealing to the new constituency, the knowledge workers.

INTERNET PROJECT

16 Find out how the U.S. president is elected. As a starting point, use the material offered under http:// bensguide.gpo.gov/9-12/election/primary.html.

6

"Federal Government"

Americans have always been critical of the size, cost and power of the federal government. The two great political parties, the Democrats and the Republicans, are divided over this issue as can be seen in the statements made by two leading officials, Phil Gramm (R-Texas) and Richard Gephardt (D-Missouri). "Should the Federal Government Be Drastically Cut?", *Scholastic Update* (1 September 1995), p.9.

1 I heartily accept the motto: "That government is best which governs least"; and I should like to see it acted up to more rapidly and systematically. Carried out, it finally amounts to this, which I also believe: "That government is best which governs not at all"; and when men are prepared for it, that will be the kind of government which they will have. Government is at best but an expedient; but most governments are usually, and all governments are sometimes,
5 inexpedient.
Henry David Thoreau, *Civil Disobedience*, 1849 (New York: The Liberal Arts Press, 1952), p.10.

"Should the Federal Government Be Drastically Cut?"

Would reducing government help or hurt?
Read the quotes from two leading officials,
then our summaries of the arguments on both sides,
and decide for yourself.

YES

"It's time for America to choose: Are we going to stay on this 30-year spending spree and squander the future of our country, or are we going to change policy and save the American dream?" - Senator Phil Gramm (R-Texas)

The federal government has a few important responsibilities, like protecting the nation from foreign invaders. But aside from defense, there's little that federal government should do.

Government is too big, too powerful, and too expensive. It tramples on the rights of its citizens and strangles businesses with overregulation. Huge bureaucracies that were supposed to help solve problems have created new ones.

Social welfare programs, for example, actually hurt the people they are supposed to help. By making poor people dependent on government handouts, the government has crushed their sense of personal responsibility and taken away their incentive to get a job. Instead of lifting them out of poverty, welfare programs cause people to get stuck in a cycle of poverty. Leave charity to the churches, synagogues, and private groups. They know best what people in their communities need.

Another example of government running amok are environmental agencies. They were set up to help protect the environment. But today, they have turned into a massive bureaucracy that cranks out mindless rules. They tell property owners what they can and can't do on their own land and insist on the most expensive way to clean up a problem instead of the easiest. Businesses get so tangled up in red tape and needless expenses, they can't afford to do business.

In the past three decades, the government has racked up a huge debt - money that we must one day pay back. The government has to stop overspending. It may hurt a little at first, but we have to tighten our belts if we are going to succeed in the long run.

NO

"Rather than force disastrous cuts in programs that help our children, we need to invest more in our children's education, safety, and development. There's simply no other way we can remain a first-rate nation." - Representative Richard Gephardt (D-Missouri)

In a civilized society, everyone is entitled to a basic standard of living. Those who profit from society must return part of their wealth to help those who are less fortunate. That's what social welfare programs are for.

People lose their jobs in hard times. Single parents can't work and care for their children at the same time (unless we provide good day care). Handicapped people who can't work need help to survive. And elderly people who have paid their dues to society deserve help in their retirement. The richest nation in the world cannot allow some of its citizens to slip through the cracks.

Private charities alone can't do the job. That's why social welfare programs got started in the first place. And with an average welfare payment of $500 a month for a family of four, there's not a lot of fat to trim. Cutting welfare punishes children whose only crime was to be poor.

Some government programs exist to make life more fair. Not everyone has money, but everyone deserves a good education and decent medical care, for example. The government should continue to help needy students go to college and not cut programs like Medicare and Medicaid that help elderly and poor people afford medical care.

The government regulates business so that we can buy a car knowing it's safe, or food knowing it's not contaminated. These regulations are good for consumers and, in the long run, businesses. Likewise, the government must protect the environment because polluting industries don't police themselves. Yes, we have to pay for these advantages. But we get what we pay for.

Vocabulary

1 to act up to (v.): to carry out - **4 expedient** (n.): a quick and effective way of dealing with a problem - **5 inexpedient** (adj.): unsuitable; not likely to achieve the result one wants - **14 spree** (n.): a period of wild irresponsible fun, spending, drinking, etc. - **14 to squander** (v.): /'skwɒndə ‖ 'skwɑːndər/ to spend foolishly; to use up wastefully - **20 invader** (n.): s.b. who goes or comes into and attacks in order to take control of a country, city, etc. - **24 to strangle** (v.): to kill by pressing their throat with your hands, a rope, etc.; here: to make incapable of acting - **30 handout** (n.): s.th. given free, such as food, clothes, etc., esp. to s.o. poor - **30 to crush** (v.): to press with great force so as to break, damage or destroy - **32 incentive** (n.): /ɪn'sentɪv/ s.th. that encourages one to greater activity - **35 charity** (n.): money or help given because of kindness and generosity towards people who are poor, sick, in difficulties, etc. - **35 synagogue** (n.): a building where Jews meet for religious worship - **37 to run amok**: to go or run out of control - **38 environmental** (adj.): referring to the natural conditions, such as air, water and land, in which people, animals and plants live - **38 agency** (n.): (in the U.S.) a department of a government - **40 to crank** (out) (v.): to produce in large amounts, as if by machinery - **41 mindless** (adj.): senseless; silly - **41 property** (n.): s.th. which is owned, such as a building, a piece of land or both together - **42 to insist** (v.): to order or demand that s.th. must happen or be done - **44 to tangle** (up) (v.): to become a confused mass of disordered or twisted threads - **45 red tape** (n.): silly detailed unnecessary official rules that delay action - **48 to rack** (up) (v.): to make greater in quantity or size - **48 debt** (n.): /det/ s.th. owed to s.o. else - **50 overspending** (n.): giving out too much money in payment for s.th. - **51 to tighten one's belt**: to try to live on less money - **54 disastrous** (adj.): very bad - **57 to remain** (v.): to continue to be - **60 to entitle** (to) (v.): to give the right to do s.th. or have s.th. - **70 dues** (n.): /djuːz ‖ duːz/ official charges or payments - **70 retirement** (n.): the period after s.b. has stopped working, usu. because of age - **72 to slip** (v.): to slide - **72 crack** (n.): opening caused by breaking or splitting - **75 average** (adj.): /'ævərɪdʒ/ calculated by adding together several quantities and then dividing by the number of quantities - **77 to trim** (v.): to reduce, esp. by removing what is unnecessary - **81 to deserve** (v.): to be worthy of - **85 to afford** (v.): to be able to pay for - **88 to contaminate** (v.): to make impure or bad by mixing in dirty or poisonous matter - **90 likewise** (adv.): in the same way - **91 polluting** (adj.): making dangerously impure or unfit for use - **92 to police** (v.): to control

Explanations

Title / federal government: The Constitution of the U.S. specifically limits the power of the federal (= national) government mainly to defense, foreign affairs, printing money, controlling trade and relations between the states, and protecting human rights. The federal government is made up of the Congress, the President and the Supreme Court. - **16 American Dream**: the idea that the U.S. is a place where everyone has the chance of becoming rich and successful. Many immigrants to the U.S. in the early 20th century believed in the American Dream. - **84 Medicare**: (in the U.S.) a system of medical care provided by the government, esp. for old people - **84 Medicaid**: (in the U.S.) a system by which the government helps to pay the medical costs of people on low incomes. It is often criticized and is generally thought to be not as good as private medical care.

AWARENESS

1 What services should a government provide? Give examples from your own life to support your suggestions.
2 Which former state services have been privatized in Germany? Find out why.

COMPREHENSION

3 What does Senator Phil Gramm refer to when he talks about "this 30-year spending spree"?
4 Why is Gramm so critical of bureaucracy and regulation?
5 Why does Gramm think there is a "cycle of poverty"?
6 What, according to Gramm, are the reasons for the inefficiency of environmental agencies?
7 Why does Gramm want the government to stop overspending?
8 What does Representative Richard Gephardt suggest to secure America's status as a first-rate nation?
9 What does Gephardt mean when he says that "everyone is entitled to a basic standard of living"?
10 Who should benefit from welfare programs?
11 Why, according to Gephardt, should government regulate business?

ANALYSIS

12 The text contains several idiomatic phrases which mean something different from the literal meanings of the words from which they are formed, for example, "... we have to tighten our belts..." (l. 51). Find other examples and explain them in their contexts.
13 Make a list of all the items and arguments that show the polarity between the standpoints expressed in the quotes from the two officials and in the two summaries.

14 The suggestion to "leave charity to the churches, synagogues and private groups" refers to the American tradition of volunteerism, i.e. helping people through privately-initiated rather than government-sponsored activities. To what extent do you think can volunteerism replace government services to cover community needs? Give reasons for your opinion.

15 Would you support Phil Gramm's view or would you be in favour of Richard Gephardt's standpoint? Write a letter to the editor in which you express your personal opinion about the question whether the federal government should be cut or not.

PROJECT

16 In comparison with the U.S.A., people in Germany have expected and enjoyed more government services. Give examples. Some of these services have been reduced. To what extent has this development changed your and your family's standard of living? Discuss your findings in class.

7

Dirk Johnson

"A Nation Bound by Faith"

A fascinating phenomenon is the importance of religion in American society. Church atten-dance, publicly demonstrated affiliations to Bible, God, and religious institutions appear strange to a lot of Europeans who are used to more secularized forms of society. - Dirk Johnson, "A Nation Bound by Faith", in: *Newsweek* (February 24, 2003), pp.17-21.

George W. Bush and the Power of Religion

1 *Of all its national traits, America's religiosity is probably the most baffling - and infuriating - for the rest of the world. Where does it come from? Why do Americans think they're on the side of right?*
5 *And why it will not go away.*

With her nation at the brink of war, Anne Summers is searching for answers. The 35-year-old software engineer follows the debate over Iraq. But like a lot of Americans, she also does something else. She prays. So 10 it was, on a frigid Wednesday night, that she trudged out to a prayer service at Willow Creek Community Church in the affluent Chicago suburb of South Barrington. One of the nondenominational "megachurches" that have proliferated in American 15 suburbs in recent years, Willow Creek looks like a corporate conference center. No crosses, no stained-glass windows, no pews. Willow Creek holds its services in a 4,500-seat, theater-style auditorium. There is even a video café, where congregants sip coffee and watch 20 services on closed-circuit television.

This day, 3,000 people turn out, most of them white, well-educated and suburban. A giant video screen displays the words OUR FATHER. Summers had prayed it would not come to this, but she supports the war even so. "Bush and Powell and all those guys are Christian," 25 she says. "I do believe that God has blessed this country."

When it comes to matters of might and right, Americans look to the heavens in a way that bewilders much of the rest of the world - especially Europe. A majority of Americans say religion shapes their lives 30 and it clearly shapes politics. Regular churchgoers are far more likely to vote Republican than Democratic, according to polls, and it's well known that the religious right is the Bush administration's political base. The president himself sometimes sounds like the nation's 35 commander in the pulpit. His State of the Union address last month repeatedly invoked divine power, declaring confidence in the "loving God behind all of life and all of history." "May He guide us now," George W. Bush beseeched. 40

The president has never shied from talking about his own embrace of born-again Christianity, at 39, a transformation, that he says helped him kick a drinking

problem. Bush attends regular Bible-study sessions in the White House. Others around him do the same; Attorney General John Ashcroft begins every business day with a prayer meeting. After a California court ruled the Pledge of Allegiance violated the constitutional separation of church and state for declaring "one nation under God," indignant politicians filed out of the Capitol and loudly recited the pledge.

Invoking the Almighty is common among American politicians, who know well that voters in the United States prefer leaders who side with the angels. But with Bush, religious conservatives can for the first time fully claim one of their own in the White House. What detractors - at home as well as abroad - find most alarming is the president's tendency to blur the lines between personal faith and policy. In fact, the White House often deliberately infuses its message with Biblical overtones. Bush's famous denunciation of the Axis of Evil - Iraq, Iran and North Korea - was originally penned as the "Axis of Hatred." The change came about, according to former speechwriter David Frum, when senior White House staff opted for a more "theological" formulation. "If people want to know me," Bush said during his campaign for president, "they've got to know that's an integral part of my life - my acceptance of Christ."

Faith increasingly seems to affect the administration's decisions. Just last week the president named a doctrinaire Christian, Dr. W. David Hager, as head of an advisory committee on reproductive-health issues for the Food and Drug Administration. Hager, who describes himself as pro-life, refuses to prescribe contraceptives to unmarried women and has written that women should treat premenstrual syndrome by reading the Bible and praying. In the Congress, the House Republican whip, Tom DeLay, refers to disputed Middle East territories as Judea and Samaria, as they were known in the Bible. Last year House Majority Leader Dick Armey suggested that Israel is entitled to the West Bank, on Biblical grounds, and that "Palestinians should leave," a claim he later tried to qualify.

Such religious rhetoric is not as out of step as it may seem. According to polls, 80 percent of Americans say a belief in God shapes their views. Conservative, evangelical churches have seen strong growth across the country in recent years, while more liberal denominations struggle to fill their pews. A popular wristband reads WWJD, or "What would Jesus do?" Many Americans today want prayer in schools and sex-education campaigns to consist solely of teaching abstinence. The Boy Scouts of America excludes gays and atheists. Pro-football players point to heavens in gratitude for scoring a touchdown, then praise Jesus in postgame television interviews.

From across the sea, it might seem that the United States is a nation of religious zealots, united in crusade. The truth is that America itself is divided. Fewer than half of all Americans attend church regularly. Much of the country, like Europe, is growing more secular, especially on the coasts and in the metropolitan centers of the upper Midwest. These are the regions where Al Gore prevailed in the 2000 presidential election – and which in fact gave him a plurality of votes. Even among the faithful, religion scarcely speaks with a single voice, especially when it comes to war. Polls show the nation is largely split on attacking Bagdhad, and opponents of war, too, often draw on faith.

And in the shaping of American values, there is more than God in the details. Capitalism, like sports – a sort of secular religion in America – takes as an article of faith that competition is the fairest arbiter, a way to yield winners and losers. Americans may see war as a last resort, but it is a resort - a decisive way to settle a contest. As Robert Cagan, of the Carnegie Endowment for International Peace, has noted, Americans see the military as a perfectly acceptable tool of foreign policy.

Europeans may cringe at the "cowboy ways" of President Bush. But in America, the cowboy is sacred in the nation's mythology, a symbol of youth, strength and self-reliance. Capital punishment, seen as barbaric in most other Western societies, derives from the time-honored code of frontier justice. Bad people - including leaders like Saddam Hussein - need to be hunted down and dealt with harshly. It is not a matter of might for its own sake, or even necessarily for narrow self-interest. Americans tend to see their country as being on the side of mercy and righteousness. What is good for America, the thinking goes, is good for the rest of the world, whether it realizes it or not.

This notion of American exceptionalism was the underpinning of Manifest Destiny, the mid-19th-century idea that America had a right and duty to extend its reach of power. The self-image of benevolence, with regard to international affairs, was burnished by America's role in the two world wars of the 20th century. Given that Americans sent millions of men to fight tyranny in Europe, and then helped rebuild war-ravaged nations, the voices of pacifism coming from the Continent ring painfully hollow.

Many Americans agree with the White House that the looming war with Iraq is a battle against tyranny, a righteous act of liberating an oppressed people. "When Americans see a picture of a woman who is suffering, they say simply, 'I want to help'," says Zainab Salbi, a 33-year-old Iraqi immigrant who founded Women for Women in Washington. "This is not something I see in the rest of the world." The flip side of that generosity, she adds, is the sometimes naive view that America "can fix everything - and always knows best." Benevolent or arrogant, perhaps some of both, Americans are praying for peace in the eleventh hour. But their faith may also bring them war.

The Relationship between Church and State

"There is no country in the world where the Christian religion retains a greater influence over the souls of men than in America."
Alexis de Tocqueville (1831)

The inscription on the dollar bill: "In God we Trust"

The President swears his oath on the Holy Bible.

As strange as it may seem - considering the above quotations and examples - there is a clear-cut separation of church and state in the US, also called the "Wall of Separation", which is based on the First Amendment.

"Congress shall make no law respecting an establishment of religion, or prohibiting the free exercise thereof; or abridging the freedom of speech, or of the press; or the right of the people peaceably to assemble, and to petition the Government for a redress of grievances."
First Amendment

This First Amendment to the American Constitution - also referred to as the "Establishment Clause" - was interpreted by Justice Hugo Black.

"Neither a state nor the Federal Government can set up a church. Neither can pass laws which aid one religion, aid all religions, or prefer one religion over another. Neither can force nor influence a person to go to or to remain away from church against his will or force him to profess a belief or disbelief in any religion. No person can be punished for professing religious beliefs, for church attendance or non-attendance. [...] Neither a state nor the Federal Government can participate in the affairs of any religious organizations or groups and vice versa. In the words of Jefferson, the clause against establishment of religion by laws was intended to erect 'a wall of separation' between Church and State."

The intention of the "establishment clause" was to separate religious activity and civil authority completely and permanently. Even if a religious group is considered dangerous by whoever, it will be protected by this constitutional right.
The Supreme Court has repeatedly ruled that a person's faith is no concern of the state.

Vocabulary

13 nondenominational (adj.): not relating to one particular religion or religious group - **14 to proliferate** (v.):to increase and spread quickly - **17 pew** (n): a long wooden seat in a church - **19 congregants** (n.): people coming together for worship - **20 closed-circuit television**: a system of cameras and television used in public buildings usually for safety reasons - **36 pulpit** (n.): a raised structure inside a church at the front that a priest or minister stands on giving a sermon - **37 to invoke divine power**: to refer to God to justify your views, to ask for God's support - **40 to beseech**, besought, besought or beseeched, beseeched (v.):(lit.)to eagerly and anxiously ask s.o. for s.th., to beg - **50 indignant** (adj.) : angry and surprised because you feel insulted or unfairly treated - **57 detractor** (n.): s.o. who says bad things about s.o.; harsh critic - **58 to blur** (v.): to make the difference less clear - **70 doctrinaire** (adj.): /ˌdɒktrɪˈneə ‖ -ˌdɑːktrɪ̩ˈner/ certain that your beliefs are absolutely true and unwilling to change them or to make compromises - **71 advisory** committee (n.): advice-giving group of experts - **98 zealot** (n.): /ˈzelət/ s.o. who has extremely strong beliefs and is extremely eager to make other people share them - **98 crusade** (n.): a strong attempt to change s.th. because you think you are morally right, campaign - **101 secular** (adj.): not connected with or controlled by a church or religious authority - **104 to prevail** (v.): to be successful, win the upper hand - **113 arbiter** (n.): judge, referee - **113 to yield**

(v.): to help to find out, to produce a result, answer - **119 to cringe** (v.): to feel very uncomfortable about s.th. - **129 righteousness** (n.): quality of being morally good and fair; (Rechtschaffenheit) - **133 underpinning** (n.): foundation - **135**

benevolence (n.): /bɪ'nevələns/ kindness, generosity - **136 to burnish** (v.): to polish s.th. until it shines - **139 war-ravaged** (adj.): very badly damaged by war - **143 to loom** (v.): to happen almost certainly and very soon

Pledge of Allegiance

The American citizens' promise to respect the U.S.A. and be loyal to it. It is made each morning at American schools and often on formal public occasions. People look at the flag and put their right hands over their hearts while proclaiming: I pledge allegiance to the flag of the United States of America, and to the republic for which it stands, one nation under God, indivisible, with liberty and justice for all.

The phrase "under God" has become a legal issue since in June, 2002, a divided three-judge panel of the U.S. Circuit Court of Appeals for the Ninth Circuit, a regional court, ruled in Newdow vs. U.S. Congress that the inclusion of these words violated the First Amendment to the Constitution. This ruling caused spontaneous protests and Congress reaffirmed the words as part of the Pledge. In June 2004 the Supreme Court left the traditional Pledge intact. In September 2005 a federal judge, however, decided that school children attending public schools should not be obliged to articulate the disputed phrase, a ruling that ignited further protest and litigation.

Explanations

72 reproductive-health issues: medical fields relating to sexuality, family-planning, pregnancy - **72 Food and Drug Administration**: Consumer Protection and Health Agency - **74 pro-life** (adj.): opposed to abortion, (opposite:) pro-choice - **77 House Republican whip**: the Republican member of the House of Representatives who is responsible for making sure that the members of the party attend and vote - **116 The Carnegie Endowment for International Peace**: founded in 1910, private, nonprofit, nonpartisan organization dedicated to advancing cooperation between nations, promoting international engagement by the United States.

AWARENESS

1 What role has religion played in your upbringing and what does it mean to you now?

COMPREHENSION

2 Skim through the article and say what the American attitude toward war is like.
3 Outline the different examples given in the text which show the close relation between everyday life and religion.
4 Describe President Bush's attitude toward religion and church.
5 What is meant by "...the President's tendency to blur the lines between personal faith and policy"?
6 What does the cowboy image of G. W. Bush have to do with S. Hussein?
7 What political consequences of the U.S.-American attitude toward religion are described in the text?

ANALYSIS

8 Examine George Bush's connection to religion and church and find out in how far it influences the political life in the U.S.A.. Use your findings from above (task 5).
9 What does the description of the church Anne Summers attends evoke?
10 In how far does the text present an ambivalent picture of religion in the U.S.? Refer to the Info Box on p. 25.

OPINION

11 Comment on the attitudes and concepts of Dr. W. David Hager, Tom DeLay and Dick Armey.

PROJECT

12 There has been a new religious wave in Europe, especially since the death of Pope John Paul II. Try to explore if there is anything like a new religious youth culture in Germany.
13 Write a newspaper article in which you explain the relationship of state and church in Germany to an American audience.

Joanne M. Marshall

8 "Religion and Education: Walking the Line in Public Schools"

World events, increasing diversity in the classroom, and headlines about the latest court cases all ensure that religion will remain a sensitive and sometimes contentious issue in the public schools. Ms. Marshall challenges readers to think about how they would respond to 12 hypothetical classroom situations involving religion. - Joanne M. Marshall, "Religion and Education: Walking the Line in Public Schools", in: *Phi Delta Kappan: The Professional Journal for Education* No.3 (November 2003), pp. 239-242.

1 In recent years religion has moved out of the private sphere and into the public square. Whether it's the invocation for God to bless America, the sudden interest in Islam, or the tale of Alabama Judge Roy Moore and
5 the Ten Commandments, religion and its impact on our world have become less private and more public. Therefore, teachers who wish to involve their students with the world around them must also address religious topics in their classroom.

10 However, issues related to religion generally make teachers very nervous. Teachers continue to struggle to observe the line between private and public expression and between church and state. This line has usually been marked by legal decisions, and no one wants to be the
15 cause of a lawsuit. Fortunately, there are several resources available to assist teachers who are uncertain about how to teach sensitive religious topics and what they can say about their own religious beliefs. [...] To test your own knowledge of where the line is currently drawn, try the
20 following 12-question self-test. Are the following actions on the part of teachers and students okay or not okay?

1. A Jewish teacher lectures on the Five Pillars of Islam.

2. During a class discussion of the U.S. role in the
25 Middle East, two students claim that the U.S. is obligated to "protect the Holy Land because America is a Christian nation."

3. During a unit on the American civil rights movement, a teacher assigns a group of students to research the
30 role of the church in African American life.

4. A student brings a Bible to class every day and reads it silently during free reading time.

5. A student wears a T-shirt to class that reads, "Hell will keep you warm" on the front and "Are you
35 saved?" on the back.

Pledge of Allegiance – One Nation Under God?

6. In response to an essay prompt asking students to write about the most influential person in their lives, a number of students write about Jesus.

7. In response to a speech prompt that asks students to give a seven-minute speech about the most influential 40 person in their lives, one student talks about the Dalai Lama and Buddhist teachings.

8. A Muslim girl wears a head covering (hijab) to class.

9. A teacher tells his class that he is fasting for Ramadan.
45

10. A teacher has a calendar on her desk with Bible verses on each page.

11. After polling her class and finding that all of the students identify themselves as Christian, a teacher holds a party on the last day of school before winter 50 break and plays Christmas music at it.

12. A teacher tells students who are being rude to one another that they have a moral obligation to be good and kind to one another.

Vocabulary

Intro/2 contentious (adj.): provoking a lot of argument and disagreement - **2 public square** (n.): forum, a large open area in the centre of a town or city - **36 prompt** (n.): *here:* topic, theme, assignment

Explanations

4 Alabama Judge Roy Moore and The Ten Commandments: a typical legal case relating to the boundary between religion and state. Alabama Chief Justice Roy Moore was suspended pending the outcome of an ethics complaint for defying a federal court order to remove a Ten Commandments monument from the rotunda of the Alabama Supreme Court in August 2003. In October 2004 the U.S. Supreme Court dismissed the appeal of former Alabama Chief Justice Roy Moore - **22 The Five Pillars Of Islam**: faith or belief in the Oneness of God and the finality of the prophethood of Muhammad; establishment of the daily prayers; concern for and almsgiving to the needy; self-purification through fasting; the pilgrimage to Makkah for those who are able - **42 Dalai Lama**: the exiled leader of the Tibetan Buddhist religion - **45 Ramadan**: the ninth month of the Muslim year, during which Muslims do not eat or drink anything during the day while it is light.

COMPREHENSION/OPINION

1 Pyramid Discussion

The following assignment is a method of focusing the discussion on the most controversial and most interesting problems rendered. It requires the student to understand the issues concerned.

As the above text presents 12 actions/questions which may be considered acceptable or rather questionable, decide on your own which three of them you categorize as okay and which as not okay. Then join in pairs and agree on two points each.

Pairs go together to make small groups. The group must also consent, but this time one single point for each category will do.

Finally the groups come up with their decisions and present their different findings. If possible identify particular questions you all agree or disagree on.

At all stages you must argue the case and give reasons for your choice.

ANALYSIS

2 Compare the results of your discussion with the suggested answers provided in the Resource Book. Concentrate on those you would not have expected.

OPINION

3 Comment on one of the answers which differs a great deal from your personal conviction.

INTERNET PROJECT

4 By using Internet sources do some research on conflicts between state and church in Germany. Take into consideration the *Kopftuchurteil* and the *Kruzifixurteil*.

For a starting point you can use the following Internet sources:

www.gegenstandpunkt.com/gs/03/04ludin.htm. ; www.dreigliederung.de/essays/1995-05-001.html.

| Art Buchwald |

"School Prayers"

The most emotional issue of the controversy concerning the relationship between church and state is that of the school prayer. Above all in times of Republican administrations and Republican Congress majorities there are passionate attempts of the influential Religious Right, an influential nondenominational conservative interest group called the Christian Coalition of America, to allow, even to lead students in prayer at public schools. - Art Buchwald, *While Reagan Slept* (Boston: G. K: Hall & Co., 1984), pp. 220-223.

1 It is to the President's credit that with all the things on his plate, including unemployment, a tough budget fight, the Falkland crisis, and his efforts to try to close the "Window of Vulnerability", he would take time to
5 propose a constitutional amendment to permit prayers in school.

Critics have accused Mr. Reagan of raising the issue at this moment as a sop to his right-wing supporters, who feel the President has been spending too much time on the country's financial problems and not enough 10 energy on the real issues facing the nation, of which school prayer is one with the highest priority.

Whether a constitutional amendment is a solution is up for debate. I believe we should try some other remedies first to satisfy everybody.

The administration has come down strongly on the side of giving tax credits to parents who send their children to parochial schools. It seems to me if this law is passed, a compromise solution to the problem would be to permit children attending public schools to be bused to a religious school of their choosing in the morning, say their prayers, and then get back on the bus and go to their public school to do their work. In this way you would give American children an opportunity to pray, but you would also keep religion off state property. Those on the bus who didn't want to pray could remain in their seats and hit each other over the heads with books.

The proprayer people say the constitutional amendment is voluntary and a child will not have to pray if he doesn't want to. The antiprayer people maintain that peer pressure as well as teacher pressure will force a kid to pray whether he has the choice or not. The latter group sees this kind of scenario:

"All right, children, we will now open with a morning prayer. Those sinners who don't believe in God can either stand in the back of the room with their faces to the wall, or hide in the clothes closet.

"Come, you little Bolsheviks, hurry it up so the rest of us can get on with seeking divine guidance. Where are you going, Tom?"

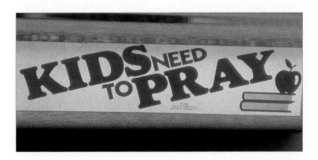

"I'm going to the back of the room. I already prayed this morning."

"And you think that's enough?"

"It's enough for me."

"Look at Tony, children. He is a perfect example of a secular humanist. He'd rather stand in the back of the room than pray to the Lord. Does anyone know where Tony is going to wind up with his attitude?"

"In Hell."

"Very good, Charles. And who will he find in Hell?"

"Satan."

"And what will Satan make him do?"

"He'll make him feed the flames of a fiery furnace, and Tony will have to wear a tail and he'll be screaming all the time and fighting off snakes, but it won't do him any good."

"That's absolutely right, Enid. Who knows what else will happen to him?"

"Blackbirds will peck his eyes out, and he'll have a stomachache all the time and his toes will drop off."

"Very good, Everett. Well, what do you have to say to that, Tony?"

"I'd still rather stand in the back of the room. "

"Are there any other Communists in the class who would like to join him? All right, Tony, you seem to be the only one. Go to the back and I don't want to see your ugly face until I tell you to take your seat. Now, class, let us bow our heads and pray for Tony's soul! Heavenly Father, there is always one rotten apple in the barrel..."

Art Buchwald was born on October 20, 1925 in Mount Vernon, New York. At the age of 17, he left high school without graduation, joined the Marines to serve with the Marine Corps in World War II. In 1948 Art Buchwald left the University of Southern California without a degree to work as a correspondent for *Variety* in Paris. The quality of his column *Paris After Dark* enabled him to become a member of the editorial staff of European edition of *The New York Herald Tribune*. When Buchwald returned to the United States he had a wide readership in Europe and the U.S.A. His humorous columns have appeared in more than 500 newspapers and magazines and have been published in more than 30 books. His international experience and his satirical style invited comparisons with Mark Twain.
He was awarded the Pulitzer Prize for Outstanding Commentary in 1982 and was elected to the American Academy and Institute of Arts and Letters in 1986.

Vocabulary

8 sop (n., usually singular): an unimportant concession to people to stop them from complaining - **39 closet** (n. especially AE): /ˈklɒzɪ̯t ‖ ˈklɑː- / *here:* wardrobe - **43 to seek**, sought, sought (v., fml.): to try to get, ask for, look for - **53 to wind up**, wound, wound (v.): to end up - **58 fiery furnace** (n.): /ˈfaɪəri ˈfɜːnᵻs ‖ ˈfaɪri ˈfɜːr-/ heated oven

Explanations

3 Falkland crisis: the war between Britain and Argentina on a disagreement about who the islands belonged to (1982). British troops reconquered the islands. - **4 Window of Vulnerability**: reference to President Reagan's Strategic Defense Initiative, a project to build a defense system in space against nuclear weapons. The plan (informally referred to as Star Wars) was renounced in 1993. - **18**

parochial school (AE): a private school which is run by or connected with a church - **41 Bolshevik**: originally s.o. who supported the communist party at the time of the Russian Revolution in 1917; before the collapse of many communist countries an insulting word for a communist or s.o. who has strong left-wing opinions.

AWARENESS

1 What is your personal opinion about prayers outside church or private homes? Does it disturb you to see people pray in public places? Would you like to pray at school?

COMPREHENSION

2 Why - according to the text - does President Reagan raise the issue of school prayer?
3 Describe the compromise the author suggests in the fourth paragraph in your own words.
4 Sum up the talk between Tony on the one side of the argument and the teacher (and the class) on the other.

ANALYSIS

5 Define the text type and examine the stylistic means employed by the author.
6 Create a dialogue in the style of this text. Invent a fictitious talk between a state official and parents on the basis of the suggested compromise from above (ll. 16-28). Start like this:
State official: "We strongly believe in the positive impact of tax credits for parents who send their children to parochial schools."
Parents: "..."

OPINION

7 Imagine you are Tony's mother or father and strongly anti-school prayer. After your son told you about the argument at school you decide to write a serious article to the local newspaper.
8 Try to put yourselves in the shoes of the teacher, who is totally in favor of school prayer. On the basis of your experience with Tony write an article to the local newspaper.

PROJECT

9 Religious Education is also a subject at German schools. Investigate the different approaches in some of our federal states. Refer to the Bildungsserver of the various federal states.

10

Dean A. Murphy

"Imagining America Without Illegal Immigrants"

The influx of immigrants - legal as well as illegal - and its effect on the host country - as much as it poses cultural challenges - is above all seen and debated in economic terms focusing on aspects such as the labor market, wage-level, consumer demand, budgetary problems on different administrative levels, welfare services, skills, and education. The controversial debate on the economic benefits and losses which is frequently backed by statistics can, however, not be settled as the figures obtained on the effect of illegal immigration are based on estimates, and their interpretation more often than not reflects attitudes and opinions. That is why Dean A. Murphy approaches this topic imagining the U.S.A. without illegal immigrants. - Dean A. Murphy, "Imagining America Without Illegal Immigrants", *The New York Times UPFRONT* (February 23, 2004), pp.14-17.

The millions of immigrants living illegally in the U.S. have long been a source of controversy. But what would life be like without them?

Try imagining America without illegal immigrants - many of the people who flip the burgers, clean the toilets, and watch the kids. Would the country be a better place?

President Bush reopened the national debate about immigration last month with a proposal to grant temporary visas to undocumented workers. His plan would let millions of illegal immigrants obtain three-year renewable work visas, if they can show that they have jobs and their employers certify that no Americans can be found to perform the work.

The announcement was the President's first big election-year policy initiative, one intended in part to appeal to Hispanics, a particularly fast-growing sector of the electorate. Bush's proposal won praise from immigrant advocates, but drew sharp criticism from many quarters.

George J. Borjas, a professor of economics and social policy at Harvard and an expert on illegal immigration, doesn't like the President's proposal. "The one good thing you could say about it is, it takes seriously the fact that the United States is not going to deport 10 million people," he says. "We have to do something about these people."

Most everyone agrees that mass deportation is unlikely. But imagining what would happen in the U.S. if the illegal immigrants suddenly disappeared is one way of understanding the economic backdrop to Bush's initiative.

Cheap Labor

The Pew Hispanic Center estimated in 2001 that the unauthorized labor force in the United States totaled 5.3 million workers, including 700,000 restaurant workers, 250,000 household employees, and 620,000 construction workers. In addition, about 1.2 million of the 2.5 million wage-earning farmworkers live here illegally, according to a study by Philip L. Martin, a professor at the University of California at Davis who studies immigration and farm labor.

That is a whole lot of cheap labor. Without it, fruit and vegetables would rot in the fields. Toddlers would be without nannies. Towels at hotels in states like Florida, Texas, and California would go unlaundered. Commuters at airports from Miami to Seattle would be stranded as taxicabs sat driverless. And home-improvement projects across the Sun Belt would grind to a halt.

"There would be a ripple effect across the economy," says Harry P. Pachon, president of the Tomás Rivera Policy Institute at the University of Southern California, a Latino research group.

But Borjas argues the disruption would not be long lasting. As proof, he says, look no further than places like

Iowa, where foreign-born residents are relatively rare, but there are people working in hotels, fast-food restaurants, and all the rest.

Most illegal immigrants, in fact, are concentrated in a handful of states - California, Texas, New York, Illinois, and Florida - leaving many parts of the U.S., relatively untouched by the influx. The Immigration and Naturalization Service estimates that 87 percent of illegal immigrants live in just 15 states.

And if there Were None ...

If there were no undocumented workers to tend to the gardening, Californians who wanted a nice lawn would pay more for it, eventually drawing low-skilled workers from other parts of the country, Borjas says, adding that American workers would be the better for it.

"The workers would be slightly wealthier, and the employers would be slightly poorer, but everything would get done," he says.

Laura Hill, a research fellow at the nonpartisan Public Policy Institute of California, says there would be a spike in prices for lettuce, spinach, and strawberries, which are typically picked by undocumented workers. But farmers and agricultural companies would eventually find cheaper ways to harvest the crops. "Who knows, but maybe it would turn into new technology being developed," she says. If not, Americans would look elsewhere, including other countries, for cheaper substitutes.

Debate over Financial Impact

Some immigration experts also suggest that American taxpayers would be better off financially if the country's illegal residents returned home. Mark Krikorian, executive director of the Center for Immigration Studies, which favors greater restrictions on immigration, argues that there would be less stress on the social-welfare system.

"Immigrants overall use at least one major program at a rate 50% higher than natives," Krikorian says, referring to an analysis of 2001 data by this center that found Medicaid use particularly high among immigrants. "That is not because they are morally defective. It is because they are poor and don't have any education, and they end up inevitably stumbling and having needs for the system."

But immigrant advocacy groups disagree. Raul Yzaguirre, president of the National Council of La Raza, a Latino civil rights organization, says the economic impact of immigration plays out differently at the local and national levels.

While hospitals and clinics in Los Angeles County, for example, bear huge health-care costs associated with uninsured illegal immigrants - one study put the total at $340 million in 2002 - the federal government enjoys a "bonanza" from many of the same immigrants who pay federal taxes but receive no benefits in return, Yzaguirre says. Contrary to popular perception, many undocumented workers do have payroll taxes deducted from their paychecks. (In some instances, undocumented workers use false Social security numbers, while others have valid numbers from when they had worked legally.)

Yzaguirre adds that without illegal immigrants, all Americans would be punished by having to pay more for everything from a McDonald's hamburger to a new house.

Blending in with Legal Immigrants

Which side to believe? The problem with gathering data about illegal immigrants - and the idea of an America without them - is that they tend to blend into the vast tapestry of legal immigrants. Someone living and working in the U.S. with a valid visa one year can become illegal the next by overstaying the visa. A single household can have both legal and illegal residents, sometimes brothers and sisters.

Patricia Nelson Limerick, chairwoman of the Center of the American West at the University of Colorado, is optimistic about President Bush's immigration proposal. "The hope is that it would lead to some recognition that you don't solve problems of illegal immigration by shutting down the border," she says, "but reckoning with the problems in the home country."

Vocabulary

5 to flip (v.): to turn s.th. quickly - **9 temporary** (adj.): limited in time - **12 to certify** (v.): to state (in a written form) that s.th. is true - **16 to appeal to** (v.): to be attractive for - **19 to deport** (v.): to make someone leave a country and return to the country they came from - **30 backdrop** (n.): background, context - **33 unauthorized** (adj.): without official or permission, illegal, undocumented - **42 toddler** (n.): a very young child who is just learning to walk - **44 unlaundered** (adj.): /ʌn'lɔːndəd ‖ -'lɔːndərd/ not washed and ironed - **45 stranded** (adj.): unable to move from a place, stuck - **47 to grind (ground, ground) to a halt** (v.): to stop gradually - **64 to tend to** (v.): to care for, to look after - **72 nonpartisan** (adj.): not supporting the ideas of any political party or group - **73 spike** (n., infml. AE): sudden large increase - **81 impact** (n.): strong effect - **85 executive director** (n.): top decision-making manager - **93 defective** (adj.): not perfect, faulty - **95 to stumble** (v.): here: to get into difficulties - **97 advocacy group** (n.): /'ædvəkəsi/ non-profit organization for public and legal support - **104 uninsured** (adj.): not covered by an insurance, without any security in case of illness, inability to work etc. - **106 bonanza** (n.): a lucky or successful situation where people can make a lot of money, a financial blessing - **109 payroll tax** (n.): a tax that is taken from someone's wages and given directly to the government - **109 to deduct** (v.): to take away an amount from a total, to subtract - **110 paycheck** (n. AE, BE: paycheque): a check that someone receives as payment for their wages; in AE also: the amount of wages someone earns;(BE): pay packet - **112 valid** (adj.): legally, officially acceptable, within a possible time-limit, correct -

121 tapestry (n.): /'tæpɪstri/ structure made of many diverse elements - **123 to overstay** (v.): to stay longer than you are allowed to, to outstay - **131 to reckon with s.th.** (v.): to take s.th. into consideration

Explanations

32 The Pew Hispanic Center: Research Center, founded in 2001, to improve understanding of the U.S. Hispanic population and to analyze the increasing influence on the American society. Its publications and Internet information are a valuable source for classroom studies. http://pewhispanic.org/about/ - **47 Sun Belt**: the southern parts of the US, where the sun shines a lot - **54 foreign-born residents**: official and statistical term referring to all the residents who were not born in the USA and including naturalized (eingebürgerte) citizens and non-citizens - **92 Medicaid**: (cf. p. 22) - **98 National Council of La Raza**: private, non-profit, and non-partisan organization focused on reducing poverty, discrimination and on improving opportunities for Hispanic Americans - **126 The Center of the American West at the University of Colorado at Boulder**: organization that brings together scholars, politicians, business people, educators, artists, ranchers, and administrators in conferences about aspects, such as multiculturalism, community building, economic and ecological issues concerning the American West: a regional fact- and think-tank.

Info

The United States
Immigration and Naturalization Service
used to be a part of the United States Department of Justice dealing with legal and illegal immigration. Since March 2003 most of its responsibilities have been transferred to agencies of the new Department of Homeland Security. The "classical" immigration services (among them the administration of temporary permanent residence, naturalization, asylum) lie with USCIS: U.S. Citizenship and Immigration Services. The law enforcement (identifying illegal immigrants, deportation, and border control tasks) has also been reorganized.

AWARENESS

1 Compile popular (or even populist) arguments in favor of drastically reducing the proportion of foreigners in Germany.

2 In which jobs – according to your impression – do you find foreign residents work?
Substantiate or modify your impression with the help of statistical (Internet) research:
See: "Ausländerbeschäftigung: Dienstleister vorn", in: *AiD – Ausländer in Deutschland: Aktueller Informationsdienst. Zu Fragen der Migration und Integrationsarbeit* (18. Jhg., Sept.30, 2002): www.isoplan.de/aid/. Here: www.isoplan.de/aid/index.htm? // www.isoplan.de/aid/2002-3/statistik.htm.
See also: Bundesanstalt für Arbeit/ Institut für Arbeitsmarkt- und Berufsforschung,"Berufe im Spiegel der Statistik": www.pallas.iab.de/bisds/erlaeuterungen.htm.

COMPREHENSION

3 Sketch President Bush's immigration proposal. State its presumable intention and reactions to it.
4 Outline the impact of doing without illegal immigrants on the American economy.
5 Reflect on the justification of the term "cheap labour" by referring to the aspects and arguments indicated in the text.
6 Explain why it is difficult to gather exact information about illegal immigrants.

ANALYSIS

7 Interpret the cartoon and relate its message to the text.

INTERNET PROJECTS

8 Compile recent data on foreign-born undocumented residents and read studies based on dates and figures.
Organize a debate on the motion:
This House believes that xenophobic reactions toward immigrants are more often based on fear than fact.
Sources: B. Lindsay Lowell, Roberto Suro, "How many undocumented: The Numbers behind the U.S. - Mexico Migration Talks", Pew Hispanic Center Report: pewhispanic.org/files/reports/6.pdf.
Jeffrey S. Passal, Randolph Capps, Michael Fix, "Undocumented Immigrants: Facts and Figures", The Urban Institute (Washington, 2004): www.urban.org/url.cfm?ID=1000587.
Michael Fix and Jeffrey S. Passal, "Immigration and Immigrants: Setting the Record Straight", The Urban Institute (Washington, 1994): www.urban.org/url.cfm?ID=305184.
Reports and surveys of the Population Division of the U.S. Census Bureau: www.census.gov/.

9 Report on the tragic destiny of the African refugees who try toget into the "fortress of Europe" via the Spanish exclaves in Marocco. Keep track of the events and the public debates in Europe. Collect material on the challenges of global migration.

11

Shannon Brownlee

"The Overtreated American"

In the United States, health-care costs continue to soar and the government is faced with the problem of reforming the system to provide all U.S. citizens with adaquate and affordable medical coverage. Shannon Brownlee points out that one of the "biggest health-care problems is that there is just too much health care" - Shannon Brownlee, "The Overtreated American" (*The Atlantic Monthly*, Boston, MA., February 1, 2003).

1 Americans enjoy the most sophisticated medical care that money can buy - and one of the most vexing health-care-delivery systems. We spend about $1.2 trillion each year, two to four times per capita what other developed
5 nations spend, yet we can't find a way to provide health insurance for 41 million citizens. After a brief respite in the 1990s when HMOs held down expenses by squeezing profits from doctors and hospitals, medical costs are once again soaring by 10 to 12 percent a year. Yet reforms
10 proposed by Congress and the White House are only nibbling around the edges of the problem.

Such political timidity is understandable, given the experience of would-be reformers of the past. Any attempt to expand coverage for the uninsured while
15 holding down costs inevitably raises fear in the minds of voters that the only way to accomplish these seemingly opposing goals is by restricting access to expensive, life-saving medical treatment. Sure, we feel bad about the 18,000 or so of our fellow citizens who die prematurely
20 each year because they lack health insurance, and about the seniors who are forced to choose between buying food and buying medicine. But Americans want nothing to do with a system like England's, which, for example, is reluctant to provide dialysis to the elderly, and most
25 of us who are now covered by either Medicare or private insurance have little stomach for health-care reform that contains even a whiff of rationing.

Behind this fear lies an implicit assumption that more health care means better health. But what if that
30 assumption is wrong? In fact, what if more medicine can sometimes be bad not just for our pocketbooks but also for our health?

An increasing body of evidence points to precisely that conclusion. "There is a certain level of care that
35 helps you live as long and as well as possible," says John Wennberg, the director of the Center for Evaluative Clinical Sciences at Dartmouth Medical School. "Then there's excess care, which not only doesn't help you live longer but may shorten your life or make it worse. Many
40 Americans are getting excess care." According to the center, 20 to 30 percent of health-care spending goes for procedures, office visits, drugs, hospitalization, and treatments that do absolutely nothing to improve the quality or increase the length of our lives. At the same time, the type of treatment that offers clear benefits is 45 not reaching many Americans, even those who are insured.

That's a sobering thought, but it opens the possibility of a new way to look at the conundrum of health-care reform. Lawmakers, insurers, and the health-care industry 50 might be able to save money if they were to concentrate on improving the quality of medicine rather than on controlling costs. Better health care will of course mean more medicine for some Americans, particularly the uninsured; but for many of us it will mean less medicine. 55

Support for this idea can be found in The Dartmouth Atlas of Health Care, a compendium of statistics and patterns of medical spending in 306 regions of the country. The atlas is generated by a group of nearly two dozen doctors, epidemiologists, and health-care 60 economists, using data from Medicare, large private insurers, and a variety of other sources. [...]

Take the regions surrounding Miami and Minneapolis, which represent the high and low ends, respectively, of Medicare spending. A sixty-five-year-old in Miami will 65 typically account for $50,000 more in Medicare expenses over the rest of his life than a sixty-five-year-old in Minneapolis. During the last six months of life, a period that usually accounts for more than 20 percent of a patient's total Medicare expenditures, a Miamian spends, 70 on average, twice as many days in the hospital as his counterpart in Minneapolis, and is twice as likely to see the inside of an intensive-care unit.

[...] Much of the variation among regions - about 41 percent of it, by the most recent estimate - is driven by 75 hospital resources and numbers of doctors. In other words, it is the supply of medical services rather than the demand for them that determines the amount of care delivered. [...]

It would be one thing if all this lavish medical attention 80 were helping people in high-cost regions like Miami to live longer or better. But that doesn't appear to be the case.

Recent studies are beginning to show that excess spending in high-cost regions does not buy citizens better health. Medicare patients visit doctors more frequently in high-cost regions, to be sure, but they are no more likely than citizens in low-cost regions to receive preventive care such as flu shots or careful monitoring of their diabetes, and they don't live any longer. In fact, their lives may be slightly shorter. The most likely explanation for the increased mortality seen in high-cost regions is that elderly people who live there spend more time in hospitals than do citizens in low-cost regions, Wennberg says, "and we know that hospitals are risky places." Patients who are hospitalized run the risk of suffering from medical errors or drug interactions, receiving the wrong drug, getting an infection, or being subjected to diagnostic testing that leads to unnecessary treatment.

An obvious way we might cut excess medical care is to change the way we pay hospitals and doctors. "Medicine is the only industry where high quality is reimbursed no better than low quality," says David Cutler, a health economist at Harvard. "The reason we do all the wasteful stuff is that we pay for what's done, not what's accomplished." [...]

Even if policymakers come up with the right financial incentives, restructuring compensation will constitute

only one small component of the reform that's needed to turn medicine into an efficient, effective industry. Think of it this way: at 13 to 14 percent of GDP, health care is the nation's largest single industry, and probably its most complex. Transforming this sprawling behemoth is going to involve a lot more upheaval than, say, the shift that took place in the auto industry when companies adopted the assembly line, or the shake-up that Hollywood and the music industry now face with the advent of Web entertainment. [...]

The last attempt at reforming the U.S. health-care system failed in large measure because of fears of rationing. Reform was viewed as an effort to cut costs, not to improve health, and voters believed, rightly or wrongly, that they would end up being denied the benefits of modern medicine. Future efforts at reform are going to have to persuade Americans and their doctors that sometimes less care is better.

Vocabulary

1 sophisticated (adj.): very well designed and very advanced and often working in a complicated way - **2 vexing** (adj.): annoying or irritating - **3 trillion** (number): one million million, 1,000,000,000,000 - **4 per capita** (Latin, adv.): by or for each person - **6 brief** (adj.): continuing for a short time - **6 respite** (n.): a short time when s.th. bad stops happening, so that the situation is temporarily better - **7 to squeeze** (v.): *here:* to strictly limit the amount of money that is available to a company or organization - **9 to soar** (v.): to increase quickly to a high level - **11 to nibble** (v.): here: to take away small amounts of s.th. so that the total amount is gradually reduced - **12 timidity** (n.): lack of courage or confidence - **14 coverage** (n.): *here:* the amount of protection given to you by an insurance agreement - **16 to accomplish** (v.): to succeed in doing s.th., especially after trying very hard; to achieve - **19 prematurely** (adv.): happening before the natural or proper time - **24 dialysis** (n.): /daɪˈælɪsɪs/ the process of taking harmful substances out of someone's blood using a special machine, because their kidneys do not work properly - **26 to have little stomach for:** to have no desire for - **27 whiff** (n.): a very slight smell of something - **28 implicit** (adj.): forming a central part of s.th., but without being openly stated - **28 assumption** (n.): s.th. that you think is true although you have no proof - **36 evaluative** (adj.): carefully considering s.th. to see how useful or valuable it is - **38 excess** (adj.): a larger amount of s.th. than is allowed or needed - **45 benefit** (n.): s.th. that gives you advantages or improves your life in some way - **48 sobering** (adj.): making you feel very serious - **49 conundrum** (n.): a confusing and difficult problem - **57 compendium** (n.): a book that contains a complete collection of facts, drawings etc. on a particular subject - **59 to generate** (v.): to produce or create s.th. - **60 epidemiologist** (n.): /ˌepɪdiːmiˈɒlədʒɪst ‖ -ˈɑːl-/ a medical specialist in the field of particular infectious diseases occurring in large numbers at the same time - **66 to account for** (v.): *here:* to make up a particular amount or part of s.th. - **72 counterpart** (n.): s.o. or s.th. that has the same job or purpose as s.o. or s.th. else in a different place - **75 estimate** (n.): a calculation of the size, amount, etc., of s.th. - **76 resource** (n.): *here:* all the medical equipment and facilities available - **80 lavish** (adj.): plentiful and generous - **97 shot** (n.): *here:* an injection of a drug - **98 monitoring** (n.): carefully watching and checking a situation in order to see how it changes or progresses over a period of time - **104 mortality** (n.): the number of deaths during a certain period of time among a particular type or group of people - **110 to subject s.o. to** (v.): to force s.o. to experience s.th. unpleasant or difficult, esp. over a long time - **115 to reimburse** (v.): /ˌriːɪmˈbɜːs ‖ -ɜːrs-/ to pay money back to s.o. who has had to spend the money because of their work - **120 incentive** (n.): s.th. which encourages you to

work harder, start new activities, etc. - **120 to constitute** (v.): to make up - **123 GDP** (n., abbr.): gross domestic product; the total value of all goods and services produced in a country, in one year, except for income received from abroad - **125 to sprawl** (v.): to spread out over a wide area in an untidy and unattractive way - **125 behemoth** (n.): /bɪˈhiːmɒθ ‖ -mɑːθ-/ s.th. that is very large and powerful - **126 upheaval** (n.): a very big change that often causes problems - **126 shift** (n.): a change in the way people think about s.th. or in the way s.th. is done, etc. - **128 assembly line** (n.): a system for making things in a factory in which the products move past a line of workers who each make or check one part - **130 advent** (n.): the time when something first begins to be widely used

---

Explanations

7 HMO: (Health Maintenance Organization) a medical service in which members receive all health care, including hospitalization, by paying a monthly or yearly fee. It has been criticized that patients can consult only doctors who are connected with the organization. - **10 Congress**: (cf. p. 14) - **10 White House**: the official Washington, D.C., residence of the President of the United States - **25 Medicare**: (cf. p.22)

AWARENESS

1 Who in Germany has to pay for the costs (doctor, medicine, hospital) when you have fallen ill?
2 Who pays the premiums for your health insurance?

COMPREHENSION

3 Why is it so difficult in the United States to expand coverage for the uninsured while holding down costs of the health-care system?
4 Sum up the main arguments which refute the assumption that more health care means better health.
5 The percentage of older people in the United States is steadily increasing. Why does this fact contribute to the rising costs of health care?
6 How could the expenses caused by excess medical care be limited?

ANALYSIS

7 Analyse the cartoon on p. 35. Explain the cartoonist's message and relate it to the statements made in the article.

OPINION

8 What is your opinion about health care?
   a) Should it be a right and not a privilege?
   b) Should everyone be given health care free of charge (for example in emergencies)?
   c) Should everyone be allowed free access to all medical facilities (for example in a Mayo Clinic)?
   d) Should the state force everybody to have a health insurance
      or
   e) should that be left to each individual?
      Discuss the pros and cons.

INTERNET PROJECT

9 Gather information about health care in Germany, Great Britain and the U.S.A. Compare the systems and point out their advantages and disadvantages. For information, consult the following websites:
www.medknowledge.de/germany/ ; http://elt.britishcouncil.pl/elt/h_what.htm ;
www.healthfinder.gov/healthcare/
Discuss what kind of system or mix of systems you would favor.

12 Karen Kornbluh

"The Parent Trap"

Karen Kornbluh, a fellow at the New America Foundation and director of its Work and Family Program, was previously the deputy chief of staff at the U.S. Department of the Treasury. In her article she compares the contemporary difficulties for families to combine work and parental duties with the situation of the post-war years, and she demands fundamental changes of social and family policies to meet the current requirements. - Karen Kornbluh, "The Parent Trap", in: *The Atlantic Monthly* (Boston, January/February, 2004), p.111-114.

**Working American parents have twenty-two fewer hours a week
to spend with their kids than they did thirty years ago.
Here's how to help the new "juggler family"**

The American family changed dramatically over the last decades of the twentieth century. In the postwar years up to the early 1970s a single breadwinner - working forty hours a week, often for the same employer, until retirement - generally earned enough to support children and spouse. Today fully 70 percent of families with children are headed by two working parents or by an unmarried working parent. The traditional family - one breadwinner and one homemaker - has been replaced by the "juggler family," and American parents have twenty-two fewer hours a week to spend with their kids than they did in 1969. As a result, millions of children are left in unlicensed day care or at home with the TV as a babysitter.

Yet the nation clings to the ideal of the 1950s family; many of our policies for and cultural attitudes toward families are relics of a time when Father worked and Mother was home to mind the children. Every time a working parent has to risk a job to take a sick child to the doctor, and every time parents have to leave their children home alone or entrust them to inadequate supervision, families are paying the price for our outdated policies.

The 1950s family is not coming back anytime soon, however, in part because the economic conditions that supported it no longer exist. Starting in the 1970s de-industrialization, corporate restructuring, and globalization led to stagnating wages and greater economic insecurity. Many women went to work to help make ends meet. Indeed, conservatives who lament that feminism undermined the traditional family model overlook the fact that the changing economic environment made that model financially impossible for most American families.

These days most women and men - across all income levels - expect to remain in the workplace after having children. Thus to be decent parents, workers now need greater flexibility than they once did. Yet good part-time or flex-time jobs remain rare. Whereas companies have embraced flexibility in virtually every other aspect of their businesses (inventory control, production schedules, financing), full-time workers' schedules remain inflexible. Employers often demand that high-level workers be available around the clock, and hourly workers can be fired for refusing overtime. Moreover, many employees have no right to a minimum number of sick or vacation days: more than a third of all working parents - and an even larger percentage of low-income parents - lack both sick and vacation leave. Though the Family and Medical Leave Act of 1993 finally guaranteed that workers at large companies could take a leave of absence for the birth or adoption of a baby, or for the illness of a family member, that leave is unpaid. This means that the United States is one of the only two countries in the Organization for Economic Cooperation and Development without paid maternity leave – the other country, Australia, is actively considering providing it.

Many parents who need flexibility find themselves shunted into part-time, temporary, on-call, or contract jobs with reduced wages and career opportunities and often, no benefits. A full quarter of American workers are in these jobs. Only 15 percent of women and 12 percent of men in such jobs receive health insurance from their employers. In other developed countries health benefits are often government-provided, and therefore not contingent on full-time employment. The United States is the only advanced industrial nation that relies on a voluntary employer-based system to provide health insurance and retirement benefits to its citizens.

Our nation has also failed to respond to the need for affordable, high-quality child care. Schools still operate on an agrarian schedule, closing at three every day and for more than two months in the summer. After-school care programs are relatively scarce, and day-care standards are uneven. (Training requirements for hairdressers and manicurists are currently more stringent than those for child-care workers.) And the expense of

Chris Slane, New Zealand, "Mothers in Workforce" (February 10, 2005)

day care - which is often more than the tuition at a state
college - is borne almost entirely by parents alone. In stark
contrast, most European nations view child care as a
85 national responsibility and publicly subsidize it. In France,
for instance, day-care centers and preschools are heavily
subsidized - and staffed by qualified child-care workers
whose education is financed by the government.

A sensible modern family policy - that supports rather
90 than undermines today's juggler family - would have
three components. The first is paid leave. No American
worker should have to fear losing a job or suffering a
reduction in pay because he or she needs to care for a
child or a parent. Every worker should be entitled to at
95 least a minimum number of days of paid leave for
personal illness or that of a family member, or to care
for a new child. In September, California adopted the first
law in the country that provides workers with paid family
and medical leave up to six weeks' worth.

100 The second component of a smart family policy is
high quality child care. The United States is practically
alone among developed countries in leaving day care
almost entirely to the private market. At a minimum,
U.S. day-care facilities must be held to higher standards
105 than they are now, and parents should be eligible for
subsidies, so that they do not have to shoulder the cost
of this care all on their own. In addition, preschool and
after-school programs should be universally available.

The third and most important component is more
110 fundamental: we should sever the link between employers
and basic benefits. In today's labor market, when working

parents need maximum flexibility and people move
frequently from job to job, it no longer makes sense to
rely on employers for the provision of health insurance
and pensions. The link between them is an industrial-era 115
relic that often denies benefits and tax subsidies to parents
who require non-standard working arrangements. We
need a new approach to our social-insurance system,
one in which control and responsibility lie with
individuals, not their employers, and in which 120
government subsidies are granted based on an individual's
ability to pay, rather than on whether he or she works
full time, part time or flex time. Unlinking benefits from
employment could do wonders for the American family:
parents could have the flexibility of part-time work with 125
the benefits that today accompany full-time work. [...]

Unlinking health care from employment could be
accomplished in a number of ways. One way would be
to expand Medicare to cover all citizens, not just the
elderly, thus creating a single-payer system. But a better 130
approach would be to create a system of mandatory self-
insurance, with government subsidies for low-income
workers and for people taking time off to care for family
members. [...]

For the past few decades both Democrats and 135
Republicans have tried to lay claim to the "pro-family"
mantle. Neither party, however, has offered a coherent
plan for giving American parents the security and the
flexibility they need. A plan that offers both would appeal
powerfully to the many voters who are having such 140
difficulty balancing their work and family obligations.

Vocabulary

Title/trap (n.): *here:* a difficult situation that can hardly be coped with - **3 juggler family** (n.): family where parents have to combine jobs and the needs for children - **9 spouse** (n., fml.): a husband or wife - **16 unlicensed** (adj.): without a licence, a document of qualification - **16 day care** (n.): looking after children or sick or old people during working hours - **20 relic** (n.): s.th. of the past - **30 corporate restructuring** (n.): new organization - e.g. downsizing - of companies - **33 to make ends meet** (v.): to manage, get by, be able to afford the bare essentials - **43 to embrace** (v., fml.): keen on accepting, be open for - **44 inventory** (n., AE): all the products in a shop, stock - **54 leave of absence** (n.): time s.o. is allowed not to work for a special purpose - **63 to shunt s.o.** (v.): to move, push s.o. - **70 contingent** (adj., fml.): depending on - **79 uneven** (adj.): not of the same quality everywhere or good in some parts and bad in others - **79 requirement** (n.): condition, regulation, results that have to be achieved in order to do or get s.th. - **80 manicurist** (n.): s.o. who cuts and polishes people's nails - **80 stringent** (adj.): strict, hard - **83 stark** (adj.): absolutely clear, harsh - **85 to subsidize** (v.): to take over part of the costs - **105 eligible** (adj.): /'elɪdʒɪbəl/ allowed to get or do s.th. - **106 subsidy** (n.): money paid by a government to reduce the cost of s.th., financial support - **110 to sever** (v.): /'sevə ‖ -ər/ to cut through s.th., to separate s.th. - **128 to accomplish** (v.): to succeed in doing s.th., to achieve - **131 mandatory** (adj.): compulsory, obligatory - **136 to lay claim to** (v.): to express that you rightfully own s.th., that you deserve s.th. - **137 mantle** (n.): role, responsibility or clothing, cover - **137 coherent** (adj.): /kəʊ'hɪərənt ‖-koʊ'hɪr-/ clear, reasonable, systematic

Explanations

58 Organization for Economic Cooperation and Development: a group of 30 countries who work together in the fields of economic and social policy to develop trade and economic growth, founded in 1961 - **139 Medicare**: (cf. p. 22)

AWARENESS

1 Interview your parents about family and work. Did they or one of them interrupt their career for your education or that of your brothers and sisters? Which organizational/ financial/ psychological efforts did they have to make to reconcile the demands of their working and family life? Give a short report to your class if your parents agree.
2 How do you feel about the impact of your parents' professional lives on family life?
   In which way has the parental professional commitment been an advantage, in which way a disadvantage for you and the family from your point of view?

COMPREHENSION

3 Contrast the American family of the postwar years with that of our time.
4 Explain why it is not possible to suggest a return to the post-war situation.
5 List the problems a working parent faces.
6 Sketch the possible solutions to free parents from the 'trap', according to the text.

ANALYSIS

7 Interpret the cartoon and relate it to issues dealt with in Karen Kornbluh's article.

OPINION

8 Debate the motion "This house believes that modern society and its work regulations and social security laws - and not the individual's 'egotism' - are responsible for a social atmosphere that is not child-friendly, and, thus, for a drop in the birth-rate."

PROJECT/ INTERNET PROJECT

9 Compare the situation of German families with that of American families as sketched in this article. Analyze the suggestions of the big American and German parties to change the situation.
   Internet sources:
   www.cdu.de/en/doc/05_07_11_Government_Programme_CDU_CSU_EN.pdf.
   "The SPD's election manifesto", in:
   www.spd.de/servlet/PB/show/1587290/280805_Wahlmanifest_kurz_englisch.pdf.
   Complete version in German:
   www.spd.de/040705_Wahlmanifest.pdf.
   "2004 Republican Party Platform", in:
   www.gop.com/media/2004platform.pdf
   "The Democratic Platform for America", in:
   http:xx a9.g.akamai.net/7/9/8082/v002/www.democrats.org/pdfs/2004platform.pdf.

13

Jennifer Washburn

"The Tuition Crunch"

Frequently German educators and politicians refer to the U.S.-American university system with its inbuilt competition, based on evaluation and ranking, and its tradition of demanding tuition fees as a model. Financial problems - due to sometimes very high fees - have been met by a complex web of public and private grant and scholarship schemes. However, it has become increasingly difficult to make ends meet as a student at a college or university. - Jennifer Washburn, "The Tuition Crunch", in: *The Atlantic Monthly* (Boston, January 20, 2004), p.140.

For low-income students college is increasingly out of reach

A four-year college degree has become all but a necessity for getting ahead in the information age. Since the 1980s the average real income of workers with only a high school diploma has fallen, while salaries among those with at least a college degree have risen: they now earn 75 percent more than high school graduates. At the national level, having a highly educated work force is critical in order to sustain our technological edge in the global economy.

College Graduates in the U.S.A.

America's higher-education system ranks among its greatest achievements. But in the past two decades our commitment to equal opportunity in post-secondary education has deteriorated markedly. In 1979 students from the richest 25 percent of American homes were four times as likely to attend college as those from the poorest 25 percent; by 1994 they were ten times as likely.

Part of the problem is the skyrocketing cost of college. Since 1980 tuition and related charges have increased at more than twice the rate of inflation, rising by nearly 40 percent in real terms in the past decade alone. Public attention has focused largely on the $35,000-plus annual cost of elite schools like Harvard and Brown. The bigger problem rests with the public colleges and universities that serve 80 percent of the nation's students. In 2003 the University of Arizona's average annual tuition rose by 39 percent, to $3,604, and Iowa State's rose by 22 percent, to $5,028. For many low-income families increases like these are difficult to absorb. Indeed, the cost for such families of sending a child to a four-year public institution shot from 13 percent of family income in 1980 to 25 percent in 2000 (for middle- and high-income families the percentage barely increased).

Congressional Republicans, led by Representative Howard McKeon, of California, contend that universities are largely to blame for these tuition hikes. However, most experts agree that fluctuations in state spending are the principal cause of tuition increases at public institutions, which depend heavily on appropriations to subsidize their operations. As Arthur Hauptman, an expert on college financing, explains, in each of the past three economic recessions - in the mid-1970s, the early 1980s, and the early 1990s - state higher-education spending per student declined, forcing students and their families to shoulder more of the cost in the form of double-digit percentage hikes in tuition. Increases during the recent recession reflect the same pattern.

The tuition spiral is not the only impediment to equality of opportunity. More significant perhaps is the nation's backsliding on need-based financial aid. In 1975-1976 the maximum federal Pell Grant award (for low-income students) covered 84 percent of the cost of attendance at a public four-year college; by 1999-2000 it covered only 39 percent. This is part of a broader shift to a system dominated by loans, which has left a generation of students struggling to finance heavy debt.

Hardest hit are low-income students, whose numbers are expected to increase dramatically over the next

decade. From 1989 to 1999 the average cumulative debt of the poorest 25 percent of public-college seniors grew from $7,629 to $12,888 (in constant 1999 dollars). Studies find that when financial-aid packages inadequately cover
70 expenses, students work long hours, attend school part time, and opt for two-year as opposed to four-year programs – all of which reduce their chances of acquiring a bachelor's degree.

Federal efforts during the past decade or so to address
75 rising tuition have done little to help low-income families. Both the Clinton and the George W. Bush administrations promoted tax breaks and saving incentives encouraging families to set aside money for college. These programs largely benefited middle- and
80 upper-income families, who have both taxable income and resources to save. With the Higher Education Act up for renewal this year, Congress should focus on aiding those students unlikely to complete – or attend – college without greater financial support, and should encourage
85 universities to do the same. To begin with, it should restore the purchasing power of Pell Grants by raising the maximum award from the current $4,050 to $8,000.

Many will argue that the cost - roughly $15 billion in additional annual spending -is unrealistic. Historically, however, our nation's investments in expanding access 90 to higher education have paid off many times over. And the money required, according to a new Century Foundation publication, is roughly equivalent to the annual revenue lost to the Treasury from tax and savings benefits that currently help those higher on the income 95 ladder. To relieve the extraordinary debt burden that many students face, Congress should also put the college-loan system under federal administration, and let every student consolidate loans and pay them off on an income-contingent basis, as one federal loan program already 100 allows.

Broadening access to higher education has never been the answer to inequality, but it *is* the way to ensure that every young person has a chance to move upward in society. Either we can continue to ignore the persistent 105 disparities in post-secondary training and rely increasingly on foreign students to fill our graduate-level science and engineering programs, or we can renew our commitment to educating the young people who are already here.

Vocabulary

Title/crunch (n.): a difficult situation caused by a lack of money - **2 college degree** (n.): the qualifications and the academic title a student gets after successfully attending an institution of higher learning - **7 graduate** (n.): s.o. who has finished an educational course - **9 critical** (adj.): important, decisive - **9 to sustain** (v.): to keep up, make s.th. continue - **9 edge** (n.): (here) advantage - **14 to deteriorate** (v.): /dɪˈtɪərɪəreɪt ‖ -ˈtɪr-/ to become worse - **18 to skyrocket** (v.): to go up, rise very fast - **36 to contend** (v.): to maintain, to state, to argue - **38 hike** (n.): rise - **42 appropriation** (n.): /əˌprəʊpriˈeɪʃən ‖ əˌprou-/ money to be used for a specific purpose - **43 to subsidize** (v.): to support financially - **52 double-digit** (adj.).; (only before noun, esp. AE): numbers between 10 to 99 (BE: double-figure) - **55 impediment** (n.): hindrance, s.th. that makes it difficult to reach a goal - **57 backsliding** (n.): falling back into a former undesirable situation or behaviour - **62 loan** (n.): money borrowed from a bank - **63 debt** (n.): /det/ a sum of money that a person or organization owes - **66 cumulative** (adj.):
/ˈkjuːmjʊlətɪv ‖ -leɪtɪv-/ increasing gradually as more of s.th. is added up - **77 tax break** (n.): a special reduction in taxes - **78 incentive** (n.): motivation, encouragement to do s.th. - **94 revenue, revenues** (n., uncountable): /ˈrevənjuː, -z ‖ -nuː, -nuːz/ money received from selling goods or services or from tax or fees - **99 income-contingent** (adj.): depending on the future income - **105 persistent** (adj.): ongoing, continuing - **106 disparity** (n) (unfair) difference

Explanations

Title/tuition (n., especially AE): the money you pay for being taught; BE: tuition fees - **13 post-secondary education**: *here:* used in the sense of higher education after the high school diploma at a community college, college or university for a first degree, usually the bachelor's degree - **58 Pell Grant award**: a federal Pell Grant can be awarded to financially eligible undergraduate students on application and - by contrast to a loan - does not have to be paid back.

Awareness

1 How do students in Germany finance their studies? What about your personal plans?

Comprehension

2 What does the text say about the development of average annual tuition costs and what does it say about family incomes in the last two decades?
3 What reasons for the current financial situation of students does the author give?
4 What are the consequences of this development?
5 What is proposed to improve the difficult situation for students?

6 Analyze the structure of the text by giving a headline to each paragraph.
7 Examine the text with regard to its function, style and tone.
8 Visualize the most important statistical figures by using bar- or pie-charts[1].

OPINION

9 Discuss the advantages and disadvantages of tuition costs with regard to equal opportunities for students.

PROJECT

10 Compare the situation of higher education as described in the text to the one you find in Germany at the moment. Make use of the following Internet source: www.studis-online.de/StudInfo/Gebuehren/.

[1] bar-chart: type of statistical visualization, especially used to compare quantities, amounts, etc. in form of columns (bars); pie-chart: type of statistical visualization, especially used to compare percentages in form of a circle (pie) divided into corresponding sections.

14 | "The Economy / International Trade"

The recession and the terrorist attacks in 2001 showed that the American economy, although strong, is not invulnerable. The war on terrorism has introduced new factors into economic decisions, including the stimulus and drain of increased defense spending, as well as the fear that military actions in the Middle East could cause oil prices to rise. Many citizens are concerned about economic policy and the long-term effects lawmakers' decisions will have on the nation's prosperity and the livelihood of current generations. - "The Economy / International Trade" in: *Current Issues*, 2003 edition (Close Up Publishing, Close Up Foundation, Alexandria, VA, 2002), pp. 78,90 and 236.

The Economy

To the majority of Americans, the economy is one of the most important domestic issues. The state of the
5 economy - including wages, inflation, job creation, and cost-of-living - plays a significant role in determining not only the strength of the United States but also the mood of its people.

Although the United States represents less than 5
10 percent of the world's population, it accounts for 21 percent of world economic output. However, it is not immune to economic troubles. After a record ten-year-long business expansion through the 1990s that brought prosperity to many households through stock holdings,
15 the American economy slipped into a recession in early 2001. The effects were compounded by the September 11, 2001, terrorist attacks on New York's World Trade Center - a symbol of American prosperity and capitalism - and the Pentagon near Washington, D.C. Furthermore,
20 a record number of companies filed for bankruptcy in 2001, some exposing corporate practices that shattered

public confidence in the business sector.

As the United States continues the war on terrorism, the effects on the economic recovery will be hard to 25 predict. Generally, wartime spending on defense and weapons boosts economies. However, the economy also depends on growth in other sectors combined with strong consumer confidence. Americans and their leaders will continue to debate the best approaches to maintaining a 30 strong economy.

International Trade

Trading goods and services with other nations is vital to the U.S. economy, and trade is a cornerstone of international relations. The end of the Cold War opened the way for increased cooperation among nations, thus creating new economic partnerships. Many members of Congress and most economists believe that free and open trade is the key to a prosperous U.S., as well as global, economy. In the last decade, Congress approved two significant free trade policies: the North American Free Trade Agreement (NAFTA) in 1993, and a General Agreement on Tariffs and Trade (GATT) accord - which created the World Trade Organization (WTO) in 1994.

Many Americans believe that the United States must restrict international trade when needed, especially with nations that abuse human rights, pollute the environment, or put U.S. goods and workers at a disadvantage at home and abroad. Proponents of free trade argue that it is the best way to strengthen the U.S. economy and to promote U.S. interests and democratic ideals in the world. When nations' enonomies grow stronger, so does their ability to protect their people and resources.

Among other trade concerns for U.S. leaders are American dependence on imported oil – deemed a security and economic risk – as well as rising concern over the role and influence of the WTO in overseeing global commerce. As U.S. and world leaders pursue opportunities to trade more freely, they will have to determine what stipulations should factor into their agreements.

Vocabulary

Intro/2 invulnerable (adj.): s.o. or s.th. that is invulnerable cannot be harmed or damaged if you attack or criticize them - **Intro/5 prosperity** (n.): when people have money and everything that is needed for a good life - **Intro/6 livelihood** (n.): the way you earn money in order to live - **14 stock** (n.): share in a company - **14 holding** (n.): s.th. which a person owns, esp. land or shares in a company - **16 to compound** (v.): to make a difficult situation worse by adding more problems - **20 to file (for)** (v.): to give a document to a court or other organization so that it can be officially recorded and dealt with - **20 bankruptcy** (n.): the state of being unable to pay your debts - **21 to expose** (v.): to show s.th. that is usually covered or hidden - **21 to shatter** (v.): here: to completely destroy s.o.'s hopes, beliefs, or confidence - **25 recovery** (n.): the process of getting better - **26 to predict** (v.): to say that s.th. will happen, before it happens - **27 to boost** (v.): to increase or improve s.th. and make it more successful - **34 vital** (adj.): extremely important and necessary for s.th. to succeed or exist - **51 proponent** (n.): a person who supports or argues in favor of s.th. - **62 to deem** (v.): to think of s.th. in a particular way or as having a particular quality - **68 to pursue** (v.): /pə'sjuː ‖ pər'suː/ to continue doing an activity or trying to achieve s.th. over a long period of time - **69 stipulation** (n.): s.th. that must be done, and which is stated as part of an agreement, law, or rule - **70 to factor** (into) (v.): to include a particular thing in your calculations about how long s.th. will take, how much it will cost, etc.

Explanations

17 World Trade Center: two buildings in Manhattan, New York City, which were the tallest in the world when they were built in the early 1970s by the New York Port Authority. The twin towers were destroyed by terrorists on September 11, 2001. - **19 Pentagon**: the large five-sided building which contains the main offices of the U.S. Department of Defense, and from which the armed forces of the U.S. are directed - **37 Cold War**: the political struggle between the U.S. and the Soviet Union after the Second World War, which was most severe in the 1950s but in the 1970s gave way to detente. By late 1991 it was considered to be over. - **43 North American Free Trade Agreement (NAFTA)**: In 1992, U.S. President George Bush, Canadian Prime Minister Brian Mulroney and Mexican President Carlos Salina established a trading partnership to lower trade barriers for industrial goods and farm products. The agreement was approved by Congress in 1993. It went into effect on January 1, 1994. - **44 General Agreement on Tariffs and Trade (GATT)**: an agreement between 76 countries which aims to encourage trade between the members - **46 World Trade Organization (WTO)**: The WTO is a global international organization dealing with the rules of trade between nations. It aims to help producers of goods and services, exporters, and importers with their business.

AWARENESS

1 Have you ever read the business section of your daily newspaper? What does it consist of?

2 Who, do you think, is interested in the information provided?

COMPREHENSION

3 What was the state of the U.S. economy like in the 1990s and in 2001?

4 What effect does America's war on terrorism have on the economy?

5 Why is the public, in general, pessimistic about the future of the U.S. economy?
6 What change in international trade took place after the end of the Cold War?
7 Why do some U.S.-Americans believe that the United States should not have trade relations with every country?
8 Why is there concern in the U.S. over the role and influence of the WTO and the issue of imported oil?

ANALYSIS

9 Make a list of all the technical terms used in this text which are related to the field of economy.
10 Analyze the cartoon. Describe what you see in the cartoon and the action taking place. Explain the message and relate it to the statements made in the article on the U.S. economy.

OPINION

11 Do you think the government should lower taxes to support economic growth? Give reasons for your answer.
12 Some people think that increasing the minimum wage would enable more people to take care of their families and to make work more attractive to those who depend on welfare benefits. Others believe that raising the minimum wage would make employers abolish jobs to pay for the higher wages of their workers and thus increase unemployment. What is your opinion?

PROJECTS

13 Find out if the main political parties in Germany have different concepts concerning the government's role in the nation's economy.
14 Working in groups, find out what kinds of American products can be bought in Germany. Why do Germans want to buy these goods?
15 Working in groups, find out what kinds of German products are exported to the United States. What makes goods made in Germany attractive to Americans?
16 Try to find out what trade agreements exist between the U.S.A. and Europe and how international relations are affected by them at present.

15

Andrew C. Revkin

"The Heat Is On"

"We must protect our environment in every community. In the last four years, we cleaned up 250 toxic waste sites, as many as in the previous 12. Now, we should clean up 500 more, so that our children grow up next to parks, not poison. I urge you to pass my proposal to make big polluters live by a simple rule: If you pollute our environment, you should pay to clean it up. [...] We must also protect our global environment, working to ban the worst toxic chemicals and to reduce the greenhouse gases that challenge our health even as they change our climate."
- U.S. President Bill Clinton in his State of the Union Address (Washington, D.C.: The White House, Office of the Press Secretary, 4 February 1997).

1 **As evidence of global warming mounts, President Bush tries to balance the environment's health with the economy's**

When it comes to global warming, who's feeling the
5 heat? One answer: most everyone on Earth. But in the sense of being pressured to act, President George W. Bush has stayed cool.

Last year, national and international panels of hundreds of climate experts agreed that most of the warming during the past 50 years has probably been caused by people, 10 mainly through burning coal and oil – creating carbon dioxide, a gas that traps heat in the air like a greenhouse roof.

The warming has intensified from the 1990s through today. The year 2001 was the second-warmest ever 15

recorded, below only 1998. This year is expected to be hotter still. If people keep pumping out billions of tons of so-called greenhouse gases each year, as we've been
20 doing for decades, temperatures could rise 3 to 9 degrees this century, many scientists say, potentially leading to the devastating droughts and floods.

The solution might seem a no-brainer:
25 Stop producing those gases and the problem goes away. Last fall, 180 nations approved the Kyoto Protocol, a treaty that would require rapid cuts in greenhouse-gas emissions. But there are deep divisions of opinion on such a global problem. One camp seeks
30 to forestall catastrophe with strict limits on pollution. The other - including the President - sees peril in doing too much.

Bush, alone among major world leaders, rejected the Kyoto Protocol, saying he would come up with a better
35 approach for the U.S. In a Valentine's Day speech, the President announced his plan. He would encourage voluntary changes for companies designed to limit, but not halt, the growth in the gas emissions. A progress report should be done in 2012, and more-stringent
40 measures might kick in, if warranted.

The environmental threat remained uncertain, Bush said, but the economic harm from rasher actions was clear. If he agreed to the stricter Kyoto proposals, Bush said, the cost to bring industry and consumers into line
45 could hit $400 billion.

Support for the President has come from a few climate scientists who think the dangers of warming are overstated, and from industries that emit lots of greenhouse gases, mainly carbon dioxide, or sell products
50 that do so, like SUVs.

But many experts say they are shocked. After analyzing Bush's policy, they say it almost guarantees a hotter future in which the ecosystems and many countries will suffer.
55 The critics include Ralph J. Cicerone, an atmospheric scientist at the University of California at Irvine, who chaired a National Academy of Science panel that provided advice to the White House last year. Cicerone says it's a mistake to use uncertainty in the science as a
60 reason to take a relaxed approach to global warming.

Continued growth in emissions of heat-trapping gases, Cicerone says, will inevitably make any risks greater. "This situation is not sustainable and its trajectory is toward dangers," he says, adding that the White House
65 proposal "lacks ambition and foresight. It sets goals that are too timid."

Finding Common Ground

One way to navigate the debate is to look first at what virtually everybody currently agrees on. No one doubts

any more that the average surface temperature on
70 Earth is rising, and that humans have, in little more than a century, increased the atmosphere's natural greenhouse effect.

Some scientists say the human influence is minimal
75 compared with natural variations in the sun's intensity and other shifts, but no one denies that humans are fiddling at least a little with the thermostat.

We've done this mainly by burning things, lots of things, to feed industrial growth: first went forests, then
80 tens of billions of tons of coal and barrels of oil, fuels that release carbon dioxide.

That gas - along with water vapor, methane, and other substances - allows sunlight into the atmosphere to warm things, but it also holds in some of the escaping heat at
85 night. If not for this natural greenhouse effect, the planet would be an ice ball. Instead, it has an average temperature of 60 degrees.

Many scientists say people have upset the normal
90 balance. Forests can grow back and absorb carbon dioxide. But once the carbon in coal and oil is released, most of the resulting gas stays in the air for decades. The result? After remaining basically constant for thousands of years, levels of carbon dioxide in the air
95 have risen 32 percent in just the last 150 years.

There is another point that everyone agrees on. Carbon dioxide makes this an extremely difficult problem to solve. It is a basic byproduct of modern life. Every coal-powered power plant, every SUV, is part of the problem.
100 Flipping on the lights, surfing the Web, doing anything with electricity contributes to it.

It's the tight link between carbon dioxide and industry that has powerfully influenced President Bush's decision. The U.S., with the world's biggest economy, is also the
105 biggest source of carbon dioxide, producing about a fourth of the global total.

Deep cuts in emissions would disrupt the economy, but allowing the economy to grow would actually help the environment, the President said. That could lead to new
110 technologies needed to end out dependence on coal and oil - technologies like safer forms of nuclear power and hydrogen fuel cells. "My approach recognizes that economic growth is the solution, not the problem," Bush said in his speech.

Waiting For A Solution

The planet can afford to wait as those technologies develop, the Bush administration and some scientists maintain. They argue that climate models predicting big changes are poor simulations on the Earth, and that the
120 atmosphere, ecology, and oceans have a large capacity to absorb the human influence. As one senior White House official says, "There is headroom."

But the Bush administration is accused of doing what's best for the energy industry, regardless of what's best for
125 the environment. Bush himself is a former oil executive who took campaign contributions from energy companies. Eric Schaeffer, a top enforcement official at the Environmental Agency, recently quit, saying he was fighting a White House that was undermining the
130 EPA's pursuit of industrial polluters. "It's this bunch of guys in energy who say, 'Boo! We don't like this,'" Schaeffer says, "and the Bush administration says, 'Well, they elected us.'"

The stakes may transcend politics. A rise of a few
135 degrees might not seem like much. But the average global temperature now is only about 5 to 9 degrees warmer than it was in the depths of the last ice age, 18,000 years ago. More warming would likely change storm and drought patterns, threatening wildlife, water supplies, and tropical agriculture, most authorities say. 140 Seas could rise a foot or more, swelled by melting glaciers and the expansion that occurs when water is warmed.

Many experts say the risk is big enough to be worth investing money now to stem the emissions that are the root of the problem, even if it costs billions of dollars. 145

"The science is already telling us that our interference with the climate is unprecedented and that we are already heading for dangerous impacts, " says Peter H. Gleick, president of the Pacific Institute for Studies in Development, Environment, and Security. "The good 150 news is that there are many things we can, and should, be doing right now to reduce greenhouse-gas emissions that are cheap, effective, and smart. The bad news is that the President's plan does none of these things."

Andrew C. Revkin, *"The Heat Is On"* (The New York Times UPFRONT, *April 8, 2002) pp.14-17*

3·1·2002 THE CHATTANOOGA TIMES

Vocabulary

Intro/3 polluter (n.): s.o. who makes air, water, soil, etc., dangerously dirty and not suitable for people to use - **Intro/5 toxic** (adj.): containing poison - **Intro/5 greenhouse** (n.): a glass building used for growing plants that need warmth, light and protection - **Intro/5 greenhouse gases** (n.): gases contributing to the greenhouse effect, i.e. the gradual slight warming of the air surrounding the earth because heat cannot escape through the upper levels - **1 to mount** (v.): to increase gradually in amount or degree - **8 panel** (n.): *here:* a group of people with skills or specialist knowledge who have been chosen to give advice or opinions on a particular subject - **12 to trap** (v.): *here:* to prevent s.th. such as gas or water from getting away - **22 devastating** (adj.): badly damaging or destroying s.th. - **23 drought** (n.): /draʊt/ a long period of dry weather when there is not enough water for plants and animals to live - **24 no-brainer** (n.): a decision that is easy and that you do not need to think about - **39 stringent** (adj.): very strict - **40 to kick in** (v.): to start or to begin to have an effect - **40 to warrant** (v.): to need or deserve - **42 rash** (adj.): doing things too quickly, without thinking carefully about whether they are sensible or not - **48 to emit** (v.): to send out gas, heat, light, etc. - **50 SUV** (n.): sport-utility vehicle, a type of vehicle that is bigger than a car and is made for traveling over rough ground - **53 ecosystem** (n.): all the animals and plants in a particular area, and the way in which they are related to each other and to their environment - **63 sustainable** (adj.): *here:* able to continue without causing damage to the environment - **63 trajectory** (n.): *here:* the events that happen during a period of time, which often lead to a particular aim or result - **65 ambition** (n.): strong desire to achieve s.th. - **78 to fiddle** (v.): here: to give false information about s.th. - **78 thermostat** (n.): an instrument used for keeping a room or a machine at a particular temperature - **83 vapor** (n.): a mass of very small drops of a liquid which float in the air, for example because the liquid has been heated - **83 methane** (n.): /ˈmiːθeɪn ‖ ˈme-/ gas that you cannot see or smell, which can be burned to give heat - **100 to flip on** (v.): *here:* to move a switch so that a machine or piece of electrical equipment starts - **107 to disrupt** (v.): to prevent s.th. from continuing in its usual way by causing problems - **112 hydrogen** (n.): /ˈhaɪdrədʒən/ a colorless gas which is the lightest of all gases, forms water when it combines with oxygen - **118 to predict** (v.): to say that s.th. will happen before it happens - **119 simulation** (n.): the activity of producing conditions which are similar to real ones, esp. in order to test s.th. - **122 headroom** (n.): *here:* freedom to do things in the way you want to - **127 enforcement** (n.): when people are made to obey a rule or law - **134 stakes** (n./pl.): *here:* risks - **134 to transcend** (v.): to go beyond the usual limits of s.th. - **141 glacier** (n.): a large mass of ice which moves slowly down a mountain valley - **146 interference** (n.): deliberately getting involved in a situation where you are not wanted or needed - **147 unprecedented** (adj.): never having happened before or never having happened so much

Explanations

26 Kyoto Protocol: In 1997, 160 nations met in Kyoto, Japan, and negotiated an amendment to the 1992 United Nations Framework Convention on Climate Change, requiring nations that ratified the agreement to lower emissions of ozone-damaging greenhouse gases. - **35 (Saint) Valentine's Day**: February 14th; on this day you send a greeting card to s.o. you love. - **57 National Academy of Sciences**: one of four organizations (the National Academy of Sciences, the National Academy of Engineering, the Institute of Medicine and the National Research Council) performing a public service by bringing together committees of experts in all areas of sciences and technologies. These experts deal with critical national issues and give advice to the federal government and the public (cf.: www.national academies.org/). - **128 Environmental Protection Agency**: the U.S. federal government organization, created in 1970, which works against pollution (cf.: www.epa.gov/) - **149 Pacific Institute for Studies in Development, Environment, and Security**: The Pacific Institute, founded in 1987 and based in Oakland, California, is a nonpartisan think-tank dedicated to protecting the natural world, encouraging sustainable development, and improving global security. Its aim is to find real-world solutions to problems like water shortages, habitat destruction, global warming, and environmental terrorism (cf.: www.pacinst.org/).

AWARENESS

1 Have you ever seriously been affected by the weather because it was too rainy, too sunny, too hot, too cold, too stormy, too humid, too dry, too unpredictable? Do you know any people who have suffered under weather conditions which had an unfavorable impact on their health or caused economic problems?

COMPREHENSION

2 What are the causes of global warming according to a majority of scientists?
3 How does President Bush justify his attitude toward the Kyoto Protocol?
4 Why is the development of our climate during the last 150 years so alarming?
5 What does President Bush mean when he says, "My approach recognizes that economic growth is the solution, not the problem"?

CARTOON ANALYSIS

6 How does the cartoonist comment on America's environmental policy?

OPINION

7 Melting polar ice-caps and glaciers, more droughts, floods and hurricanes are the effects of the increasing pollution of the atmosphere. Unless the rise in temperature can be stopped, a permanent climate change will be inevitable. Do you think that environmental protection and economic growth can coexist?
8 Supporters of the Kyoto plan argue that if a superpower like the U.S.A. takes the lead, other nations, particularly, developing countries, will follow. Opponents of the Kyoto Protocol point out that experts still disagree on how much greenhouse gases contribute to global warming and that the cost of developing new technologies could harm the economies of industrialized nations costing workers their jobs. Whose arguments do you consider convincing? Give reasons.

INTERNET PROJECT

9 Find out to what extent the hurricanes Katrina and Rita which devastated New Orleans (Louisiana) and Galveston (Texas) in 2005 have had any effect on the environmental policies of the U.S. government. Use the following website as a starting point:
www.nrdc.org/legislation/katrina/katrinainx.asp.

16 | David Lehman

"The World Trade Center"

In the immediate aftermath of the 9/11-attacks there have only been few literary works of art trying to deal with and overcome these shocking events. Apart from essays, poems became the most important medium for artistic reactions to terrorist atrocities. An anthology documents some of the most sensitive poetry on 9/11, 2001, by New York writers. Because of the total destruction of the World Trade Center David Lehman introduces this collection with a poem he wrote in 1996 about the first terrorist attack against this New York symbol that took place in 1993. - David Lehman, "The World Trade Center", from: Dennis Loy Johnson and Valerie Merians (eds.), *Poetry After 9/11* (Hoboken, New Jersey: Melville House, 2002), p. XV.

I never liked the World Trade Center.   1
When it went up I talked it down
As did many other New Yorkers.
The twin towers were ugly monoliths
That lacked the details the ornament the character   5
Of the Empire State Building and especially
The Chrysler Building, everyone's favorite,
With its scalloped top, so noble.
The World Trade Center was an example of what was wrong
With American architecture,   10
And it stayed that way for twenty-five years
Until that Friday afternoon in February
When the bomb went off and the buildings became
A great symbol of America, like the Statue
Of Liberty at the end of Hitchcock's *Saboteur*.   15
My whole attitude toward the World Trade Center
Changed overnight. I began to like the way
It comes into view as you reach Sixth Avenue
From any side street, the way the tops
Of the towers dissolve into the white skies   20
In the east when you cross the Hudson
Into the city across the Washington Bridge.

Vocabulary

4 monolith (n.): /ˈmɒnəlɪθ ‖ ˈmɑː-/ a large tall block of stone, especially one that was put in place in ancient times, possibly for religious reasons - **8 scalloped** (adj.): with a curved edge - **20 to dissolve into** (v.): *here:* to disappear into

Explanation

15 *Saboteur*: in this Alfred Hitchcock film a plant worker is falsely blamed for having sabotaged his company. He chases down the man he believes to be the real saboteur atop the Statue of Liberty.

Background Reading

September 11 Attacks   1
... series of airline hijackings and suicide attacks committed by 19 militants associated with the Islamic extremist group al-Qaeda against targets in the United States. The attacks caused extensive death and destruction and triggered an enormous U.S. effort to combat terrorism.   5

The hijackers, most of whom were from Saudi

Arabia, established themselves in the United States, many well in advance of the attacks. They traveled in small groups, and some of them received commercial flight training. On September 11, 2001, groups of attackers boarded four domestic aircraft (a 20th suspected militant had been detained by U.S. authorities) at three East Coast airports and soon after takeoff disabled the crews and took control of the planes. The aircraft, all large and bound for the West Coast, had full loads of fuel.

At 8:46 AM (local time) the terrorists piloted the first plane, which had originated from Boston, into the north tower of the World Trade Center in New York City. A second plane, also from Boston, struck the south tower roughly 15 minutes later. Each structure was badly damaged by the impact and erupted into flames. A third plane, from the Washington, D.C., area, struck the southwest side of the Pentagon just outside of the city at 9:40, touching off a fire in that section of the structure. Within the next hour the fourth aircraft (from Newark, New Jersey) crashed in the Pennsylvania countryside after its passengers - informed of events via cellular phone - attempted to overpower their assailants.

At 9:59 the World Trade Center's heavily damaged south tower collapsed; the north tower fell about half an hour later. A number of other buildings adjacent to the twin towers suffered serious damage, and several subsequently fell. Fire at the World Trade Center site smoldered for more than three months.

Rescue operations began almost immediately, as the country and the world sought to come to grips with the enormity of the losses. Some 2,750 people were killed in New York, 184 at the Pentagon, and 40 in Pennsylvania; all 19 terrorists died. Police and fire departments in New York were especially hard hit: hundreds had rushed to the scene of the attacks and more than 400 police officers and firefighters were killed.

The emotional distress caused by the attacks - particularly the collapse of the twin towers, New York City's most visible landmark - was overwhelming. Unlike the relatively isolated site of the Pearl Harbor attack of 1941, to which the September 11 events were soon compared, the World Trade Center lay at the heart of one of the world's largest cities. Hundreds of thousands of people witnessed the attacks firsthand (many onlookers photographed events or recorded them with video cameras), and millions watched the tragedy unfold live on television. In the days that followed September 11, the footage of the attacks was replayed in the media countless times, as were the scenes of throngs of people, stricken with grief, gathering at "ground zero" - as the site where the towers once stood came to be known - some with photos of missing loved ones, seeking some hint of their fate.

Moreover, world markets were badly shaken; the towers were at the heart of New York's financial district, and damage to Manhattan's infrastructure, combined with fears of stock market panic, kept New York markets closed for four trading days. Markets afterward suffered record losses.

Countries allied with the United States rallied to its support. Evidence gathered by the United States soon convinced most governments that the Islamic militant group al-Qaeda was responsible for the attacks. The group had been implicated in previous terrorist strikes against Americans, and its leader Osama bin Laden had made numerous anti-American statements. Al-Qaeda was headquartered in Afghanistan and had forged a close relationship with that country's ruling Taliban militia, which subsequently refused U.S. demands to extradite bin Laden and to terminate al-Qaeda activity there. In early October, U.S. and allied forces launched an attack that, within months, killed or captured thousands of militants and drove Taliban and al-Quaeda leaders into hiding.

After September 11 the U.S. government exerted great effort to track down other al-Qaeda agents and sympathizers throughout the world, and it made combating terrorism the focus of U.S. foreign policy. Meanwhile, security measures within the country were tightened considerably at such places as airports, government buildings, and sports venues.

"September 11 attacks", in: Encyclopaedia Britannica Online *(accessed 2 Dec. 2004);* http:xx search.eb.com/eb/article?ocld=9394915.

Vocabulary

6 to trigger (v.): to make s.th. happen very quickly, to initiate - **7 to combat** (v.): to try to stop s.th. bad from happening or getting worse, to fight against - **13 to board** (v. fml.): to get on a plane, boat etc. - **13 domestic** (adj.): within one country - **14 suspected** (adj.): s.o. who is thought to be guilty of a crime - **14 to detain** (v.): to officially prevent s.o. from leaving a place - **16 to disable s.o.** (v.): to make s.o. unable to move - **17 bound for** (adj.): travelling to - **23 to strike, struck, struck** (v.): to hit - **32 to overpower** (v.): to take control of s.o. physically because you are stronger - **35 adjacent** (adj.): /ə'dʒeisənt/ next to - **37 subsequently** (adv.): after an event, afterwards, then - **38 to smolder** (v.): to burn slowly without a flame - **40 to seek, sought, sought to** (v.): to try to - **40 to come to grips with** (v.): to deal with s.th. difficult - **48 distress** (n.): a feeling of great unhappiness and pain - **58 to unfold** (v.): to happen, to develop - **59 footage** (n.): film showing a particular event - **61 throng** (n.): crowd - **61 stricken** (adj.): very badly affected, suffering extremely - **62 grief** (n.): extreme sadness, especially because s.o. you love has died - **72 to rally** (v.): to come together, join - **76 to be implicated** (v., fml., usually passive): to be the cause, to be decisively involved in s.th. bad or harmful - **80 to forge** (v.): to build up, esp. a strong relationship - **82 to extradite** (v.): /'ekstrədait/ to send s.o. who may be guilty of a crime to the country where the crime happened in order to have a trial - **84 to launch** (v.): to start - **94 venue** (n.): a place where sporting events, concerts etc. take place

Andrea Carter Brown

"The Old Neighborhood"

The following poem by Andrea Carter Brown indicates subtly that cultural diversity had become a matter of course before the terrorist attacks of 9/11, 2001. It is a poem of grief and mourning for missing individuals of this multicultural city,and it evokes a sense of solidarity between the diverse ethnic groups. - Andrea Carter Brown, "The Old Neighborhood", in: Dennis Loy Johnson and Valerie Merians (Eds.), *Poetry After 9/11* (Hoboken, New Jersey: Melville House, 2002), pp. 7-8.

1 Where is the man who sold the best jelly donuts and coffee
you sipped raising a pastel blue Acropolis to your lips? Two

brothers who arrived in time for lunch hour with hot and cold
heroes where Liberty dead ends at the Hudson? The courteous

5 small-boned Egyptian in white robe and crocheted skullcap
in the parking lot behind the Greek Orthodox shrine whose

bananas and dates you could always count on? How about
the tall, slim, dark brown man with dreadlocks cascading

to his waist who grilled Hebrew National franks to perfection
10 and knew just the right amount of mustard each knish wanted?

The cinnamon-skinned woman for whose roti people lined up
halfway down Church, the falafel cousins who remembered

how much pepper you preferred? Don't forget the farmers
who shlepped up from Cape May twice each week at dawn

15 to bring us whatever was in season at its peak: last August,
blueberries and white peaches. What about the lanky fellow

who sold green and red and yellow bears and fish and snakes
in plastic sandwich bags with twist ties; his friend, a block

away, who scooped still warm nuts from a silver cauldron
20 into palm-sized wax paper sacks the twisted at the corners

to close? The couple outside the post office with their neatly
laid out Golden Books, the shy Senegalese with briefcases

of watches except in December when they sold Christmas
trees? The Mr. Softee who parked every evening rush hour

25 by the cemetery to revive the homeward hurrying crowd?
I know none of their names, but I can see their faces clear

as I still see everything from that day as I ride away from
the place we once shared. Where are they now? And how?

Vocabulary

1 jelly (n.): a thick sweet substance made from boiled and sugar - **1 donut/ doughnut** (n.): /ˈdəʊnʌt ‖ ˈdoʊ-/ a small round cake, often in the form of a ring - **4 hero** (n., AE): a long thin sandwich filled with meat, cheese etc - **4 to dead end** (v., here poetic functional shift): hit upon - **4 courteous** (adj.): /ˈkɜːtɪəs ‖ ˈkɜːr-/ polite - **5 robe** (n.): a long loose piece of clothing - **5 to crochet** (v.): to make clothes from wool or cotton using a special needle with a hook at one end (häkeln) - **5 skullcap** (n.): a small round close-fitting hat for the top of the head - **7 date** (n.): a sweet sticky brown fruit with a long hard seed inside - **8 dreadlocks** (n.): a way of arranging your hair, popular with Rastafarians, in which it hangs in thick pieces that look like rope - **8 to cascade** (v.): to flow, fall, or hang down in large quantities - **11 cinnamon** (n.): a sweet-smelling brown substance used for giving a special taste to cakes and other sweet foods - **14 to shlep** (v., infml. AE): /ʃlep/ to carry or pull s.th. heavy

- **16 lanky** (adj.): tall and thin, moving awkwardly - **19 to scoop** (v.): to pick s.th. up or remove it using a scoop or a spoon, or your curved hand - **19 cauldron** (n.): /ˈkɔːldrən ‖ ˈkɒːl-/ a large round metal pot for boiling liquids over a fire - **20 palm** (n.): the inside surface of your hand - **25 to revive** (v.): to make s.o. healthy and strong again

Explanations

10 knish: Eastern European Jewish or Yiddish snack food - **11 roti**: type of Indian bread - **9 Hebrew National franks**: here: Jewish style sausages (frankfurters) - **12 falafel** (n.): fried balls of an Arabic food made with large brown peas (chickpeas) - **18 twist ties** (n.): mainly thin plastic ties to close a small plastic or paper bag containing food

David Lehman was born in New York City in 1948. He has published five books of poetry as well as numerous important books of criticism. He is the editor of the annual anthology of *The Best American Poetry*. His honors include fellowships from the Guggenheim Foundation and the National Endowment for the Arts. Apart from writing, he teaches at Bennington College and the New School for Social Research, New York City.

Andrea Carter Brown, the author of poetry books – *Brooke and Rainbow* (2001) and *The Disheveled Bed* (2005) – was temporarily replaced from her home in Battery Park by the events of September 11. She meanwhile moved to California, where she contributes to the *Emily Dickinson Journal* at Pomona College as the managing editor. She is also committed to teaching poetry.

AWARENESS

1 There are moments of history that leave a deep impression on people - the terrorist attacks on New York and Washington on 9/11, 2001, belong to this category. Try to remember what you were doing when you learnt about these events. Describe your emotions, your thoughts.
Interview older friends or your parents about their reactions to 9/11, 2001. Ask them whether they feel that the world has changed since then.

2 List examples of terrorist attacks; find out who were the (presumable) perpetrators, who the victims. Describe the impact of these attacks.

COMPREHENSION

3 Sum up the information of the encyclopaedic article and give your summary the form of an entry into a students' encyclopaedia of American studies.

ANALYSIS

4 Interpret David Lehman's "The World Trade Center" and Andrea Carter Brown's "The Old Neighborhood" and compare them to each other.

CREATIVE WRITING

5 Formulate diary entries or poems on terrorist acts you remember.

17

Statement from American Scholars Supporting the U.S. Government's War on Terrorism

In February 2002, 58 renowned scholars of various disciplines and comprising the entire democratic spectrum of the United States published and signed a manifest that provides ethical, political, and legal arguments justifying the war on terrorism wedged at that time upon the Taliban regime in Afghanistan. The manifest was endorsed in the United States of America, whereas it was controversially discussed in the Federal Republic of Germany. Whatever the individual political reaction to the content may be, its language and structure is complex, differentiated, and far from a simplistic justification of war. - Institute of American Values, www.americanvalues.org, (New York, February 12, 2002).

What We're Fighting For
A Letter from America

1 At times it becomes necessary for a nation to defend itself through force of arms. Because war is a grave matter, involving the sacrifice and taking of precious human life, conscience demands that those who would
5 wage the war state clearly the moral reasoning behind their actions, in order to make plain to one another, and to the world community, the principles they are defending.

We affirm five fundamental truths that pertain to all
10 people without distinction:
1. All human beings are born free and equal in dignity and rights.
2. The basic subject of society is the human person, and the legitimate role of government is to protect and
15 help to foster the conditions for human flourishing.
3. Human beings naturally desire to seek the truth about life's purpose and ultimate ends.
4. Freedom of conscience and religious freedom are inviolable rights of the human person.
20 5. Killing in the name of God is contrary to faith in God and is the greatest betrayal of the universality of religious faith.

We fight to defend ourselves and to defend these universal principles.

What are American values? 25

Since September 11, millions of Americans have asked themselves and one another, why? Why are we the targets of these hateful attacks? Why do those who would kill us, want to kill us?

We recognize that at times our nation has acted with 30 arrogance and ignorance toward other societies. At times our nation has pursued misguided and unjust policies. Too often we as a nation have failed to live up to our ideals. We cannot urge other societies to abide by moral principles without simultaneously admitting our own 35 society's failure at times to abide by those same principles. We are united in our conviction – and are confident that all people of good will in the world will agree – that no appeal to the merits or demerits of specific foreign policies can ever justify, or even purport to make sense 40 of, the mass slaughter of innocent persons.

Moreover, in a democracy such as ours, in which government derives its power from the consent of the governed, policy stems at least partly from culture, from the values and priorities of the society as a whole. Though 45 we do not claim to possess full knowledge of the motivations of our attackers and their sympathizers, what we do know suggests that their grievances extend far beyond any one policy, or set of policies. After all, the killers of September 11 issued no particular demands; 50 in this sense, at least, the killing was done for its own sake. The leader of Al Qaeda described the "blessed strikes" of September 11 as blows against America, "the head of world infidelity." Clearly, then, our attackers despise not just our government, but our overall society, 55 our entire way of living. Fundamentally, their grievance concerns not only what our leaders do, but also who we are.

So who are we? What do we value? For many people, including many Americans and a number of signatories 60 to this letter, some values sometimes seen in America are unattractive and harmful. Consumerism as a way of life. The notion of freedom as no rules. The notion of the individual as self-made and utterly sovereign, owing little to others or to society. The weakening of marriage and family life. Plus an enormous entertainment and communications apparatus that relentlessly glorifies such ideas and beams them, whether they are welcome or not, into nearly every corner of the globe.

One major task facing us as Americans, important prior to September 11, is facing honestly these unattractive aspects of our society and doing all we can to change them for the better. We pledge ourselves to this effort.

At the same time, other American values - what we view as our founding ideals, and those that most define our way of life - are quite different from these, and they are much more attractive, not only to Americans, but to people everywhere in the world. Let us briefly mention four of them.

The first is the conviction that all persons possess innate human dignity as a birthright, and that consequently each person must always be treated as an end rather than used as a means. The founders of the United States, drawing upon the natural law tradition as well as upon the fundamental religious claim that all persons are created in the image of God, affirmed as "self-evident" the idea that all persons possess equal dignity. The clearest political expression of a belief in transcendent human dignity is democracy. In the United States in recent generations, among the clearest cultural expressions of this idea has been the affirmation of the equal dignity of men and women, and of all persons regardless of race or color.

Second, and following closely from the first, is the conviction that universal moral truths (what our nation's founders called "laws of Nature and of Nature's God") exist and are accessible to all people. Some of the most eloquent expressions of our reliance upon these truths are found in our Declaration of Independence, George Washington's Farewell Address, Abraham Lincoln's Gettysburg Address and Second Inaugural Address, and Dr. Martin Luther King, Jr.'s Letter from the Birmingham Jail.

The third is the conviction that, because our individual and collective access to truth is imperfect, most disagreements about values call for civility, openness to other views, and reasonable argument in pursuit of truth.

The fourth is freedom of conscience and freedom of religion. These intrinsically connected freedoms are widely recognized, in our own country and elsewhere, as a reflection of basic human dignity and as a precondition for other individual freedoms.

To us, what is most striking about these values is that they apply to all persons without distinction, and cannot be used to exclude anyone from recognition and respect based on the particularities of race, language, memory, or religion. That's why anyone, in principle, can become an American. And in fact, anyone does. People from everywhere in the world come to our country with what a statue in New York's harbor calls a yearning to breathe free, and soon enough, they are Americans. Historically, no other nation has forged its core identity - its constitution and other founding documents, as well as its basic self-understanding - so directly and explicitly on the basis of universal human values. To us, no other fact about this country is more important.

Some people assert that these values are not universal at all, but instead derive particularly from western, largely Christian civilization. They argue that to conceive of these values as universal is to deny the distinctiveness of other cultures. We disagree. We recognize our own civilization's achievements, but we believe that all people are created equal. We believe in the universal possibility and desirability of human freedom. We believe that certain basic moral truths are recognizable everywhere in the world. We agree with the international group of distinguished philosophers who in the late 1940s helped to shape the United Nations Universal Declaration of Human Rights, and who concluded that a few fundamental moral ideas are so widespread that they "may be viewed as implicit in man's nature as a member of society." In hope, and on the evidence, we agree with Dr. Martin Luther King, Jr., that the arc of the moral universe is long, but it bends toward justice, not just for the few, or the lucky, but for all people.

Looking at our own society, we acknowledge again the all too frequent gaps between our ideals and our conduct. But as Americans in a time of war and global crisis, we are also suggesting that the best of what we too casually call "American values" do not belong only to America, but are in fact the shared inheritance of humankind, and therefore a possible basis of hope for a world community based on peace and justice. [...]

Vocabulary

2 grave (adj.): serious - **3 sacrifice** (n.): losing one's life fighting for a cause - **3 precious** (adj.): valuable - **5 to wage** (war, a campaign, battle etc) (v.): to be involved in a war or a fight - **5 reasoning** (n.): the process of thinking carefully before making a decision - **11 dignity** (n.): sense of value, importance, respect deserved - **15 to foster** (v.): to help develop, encourage, promote - **15 to flourish** (v.): to develop well, healthily, be successful, to thrive - **17 ultimate** (adj.): final - **17 end** (n.): aim, purpose, sense - **19 inviolable**

right: extremely important right to be treated with respect and not broken or removed - **21 betrayal** (n.): disloyalty, act of giving up, breaking fundamental beliefs, principles - **21 universality** (n): s.th. that holds true, is valid everywhere and for everyone, - **25 target** (n): object of attack - **32 to pursue** (v.): to try to achieve s.th. over a period of time - **32 misguided** (adj.): wrong, based on a wrong understanding of a situation - **34 to urge** (v.): strongly suggest, encourage s.o. to do s.th. - **34 to abide by** (v.): to accept and obey a decision, rule, principle, to stick to - **39 merit** (n.): an advantage or good feature of s.th. - **39 demerit** (n.): a bad quality or feature of s.th. - **44 to stem from s.th.** (v.): to develop as a result from s.th. else - **45 priority** (n.): the thing that deserves attention before others, the thing (value, task) seen as most important - **48 grievance** (n.): feeling of being treated unfairly, unfair, upsetting situation - **50 to issue** (v.): to publish, to make an official statement - **54 infidelity** (n.): *here:* attitude of ignoring, not believing in a higher being - **60 signatory** (n.): /ˈsɪgnətəri ‖ -tɔːri/ a person, organization, or country that signs a document - **63 notion** (n.): an idea, belief, opinion - **64 utterly** (adv.): completely, totally, extremely - **64 sovereign** (adj.): independent, autonomous, emancipated - **67 relentless** (adj.): endless - **68 to beam** (v.): to send, broadcast - **71 prior to** (adj., fml.): before - **73 to pledge** (v.): to make a formal promise - **82 innate** (adj.): inborn, by birth, natural - **84 means** (n., plural): instrument, method - **87 to affirm** (v.): to confirm, to

strengthen a belief, an idea - **88 self-evident** (adj.). obvious - **90 transcendent** (adj.): going far beyond ordinary limits such as space and time - **98 accessible** (adj.): possible to reach or get - **99 eloquent** (adj.) - well-expressed, convincing - **106 access** (n.): right to enter a place, get s.th. etc, the way to reach s.th. - **111 intrinsic** (adj.): being part of the nature or character of s.th.; here: intrinsically connected: naturally connected - **118 particularity** (n, fml.): a quality that makes s.th. different from all others - **122 to yearn** (v., lit.): to have a strong desire for s.th., to long - **124 to forge** (v.): to form, to develop - **124 core** (adj.) most important, central, main - **132 distinctiveness** (n.): a special quality that makes s.th./s.o. different and easy to identify - **136 desirability** (n., fml.): advantage or a state that makes people wish to achieve - **145 arc** (n.): a curved shape - **148 to acknowledge** (v.): to admit - **149 conduct** (n.): /ˈkɒndʌkt ‖ ˈkɑːn-/ behavior - **153 inheritance (n.)**: tradition

Noam Chomsky

"Reflections on 9-11"

Although there was no major public controversy on the justification of the Bush Administration's national and international measures, it should, however, be emphasized that there has been a lot of self-criticism, even among those endorsing these measures (cf. pp. 52-53), and more fundamental criticism by individual intellectuals focusing on the structure of the social system in the United States. Noam Chomsky is one of the most prominent critics, whose analyses are embedded in a wider context of critical reflections on the globalization process. - Noam Chomsky, "Reflections on 9-11", in: Noam Chomsky, *9-11* (New York: Seven Stories Press, 2002), pp. 119 - 128.

1 It is widely argued that the September 11 terrorist attacks have changed the world dramatically, that nothing will be the same as the world enters into an "age of terror" - the title of a collection of academic essays by Yale
5 University scholars and others, which regards the anthrax attack as even more ominous.

There is no doubt that the 9-11 atrocities were an event of historic importance, not - regrettably - because of their scale, but because of the choice of innocent victims.
10 It had been recognized for some time that with new technology, the industrial powers would probably lose their virtual monopoly of violence, retaining only an enormous preponderance. No one could have anticipated the specific way in which the expectations were fulfilled,
15 but they were. For the first time in modern history, Europe and its offshoots were subjected, on home soil, to the kind of atrocity that they routinely have carried out elsewhere. The history should be too familiar to review, and though the West may choose to disregard
20 it, the victims do not. The sharp break in the traditional pattern surely qualifies 9-11 as a historic event, and the repercussions are sure to be significant.

Several crucial questions arose at once:
(1) who is responsible?
25 (2) what are the reasons?
(3) what is the proper reaction?
(4) what are the longer-term consequences?

As for (1), it was assumed, plausibly, that the guilty parties were bin Laden and his al-Qaeda network. [...]
Nevertheless, despite what must be the most intensive 30 international intelligence investigation in history, evidence about the perpetrators of 9-11 has been hard to find. Eight months after the bombing, FBI director Robert Mueller, testifying to Congress, could say only that U.S. intelligence now "believes" the plot was hatched 35 in Afghanistan, though planned and implemented elsewhere. And long after the source of the anthrax attack was localized to U.S. government weapons laboratories, it has still not been identified. These are indications of how hard it may be to counter acts of terror targeting the 40 rich and powerful in the future. Nevertheless, despite the thin evidence, the initial conclusion about 9-11 is presumably correct.

Turning to (2), scholarship is virtually unanimous in taking the terrorists at their word, which matches their 45 deeds for the past twenty years: their goal, in their terms, is to drive the infidels from Muslim lands, to overthrow the corrupt governments they impose and sustain, and to institute an extremist version of Islam.

[...] In George Bush's plaintive words, "why do they 50 hate us?" the question is not new, and answers are not hard to find. Forty-five years ago President Eisenhower and his staff discussed what he called the "campaign of hatred against us" in the Arab world, "not by the governments but by the people." The basic reason, the National Security council advised, is the recognition that the U.S. supports corrupt and brutal governments that block democracy and development, and does so because of its concern "to protect its interest in Near East oil." The Wall Street Journal found much the same when it investigated attitudes of wealthy westernized Muslims after 9-11, feeling now exacerbated by specific U.S. policies with regard to Israel/Palestine and Iraq.

Americans united in grief

Commentators generally prefer a more comforting answer: their anger is rooted in resentment of our freedom and love of democracy, their cultural failings tracing back many centuries, their inability to take part in the form of "globalization" (in which they happily participate), and other such deficiencies. More comforting, perhaps, but not wise.

What about proper reaction, question (3)? The answers are doubtless contentious, but at least the reaction should meet the most elementary moral standards: specifically, if an action is right for us, it is right for others; and if wrong for others, it is wrong for us. Those who reject that standard simply declare that acts are justified by power; they can therefore be ignored in any discussion of appropriateness of action, of right or wrong. One might ask what remains of the flood of commentary on question (3) (debates about "just war," etc.) if this simple criterion is adopted.

To illustrate with a few uncontroversial cases, forty years have passed since President Kennedy ordered that "the terrors of the earth" must be visited upon Cuba until their leadership is eliminated, having violated good form by successful resistance to U.S.-run invasion. The terrors were extremely serious, continuing into the 1990s. Twenty years have passed since President Reagan launched a terrorist war against Nicaragua, conducted with barbaric atrocities and vast destruction, leaving tens of thousands dead and the country ruined perhaps beyond recovery - and also leading to condemnation of the U.S. for international terrorism by the World Court and the UN Security Council (in a resolution the U.S. vetoed). But no one believes that Cuba or Nicaragua had the right to set off bombs in Washington or New York, or to assassinate U.S. political leaders. And it is all too easy to add many far more severe cases, up to the present.

Accordingly, those who accept elementary moral standards have some work to do to show that the U.S. and Britain were justified in bombing Afghans in order to compel them to turn over people who the U.S. suspected of criminal atrocities, the official war aim, announced by the President as the bombing began; or to overthrow their rulers, the war aim announced several weeks later. [...]

Let us turn briefly to these last considerations: question (4).

In the longer term, I suspect that the crimes of 9-11 will accelerate tendencies that were already underway: the Bush doctrine (of "preemptive strike") [...] is an illustration. As was predicted at once, governments throughout the world seized upon 9-11 as a window of opportunity to institute or escalate harsh and repressive programs. Russia eagerly joined the "coalition against terror" expecting to receive authorization for its terrible atrocities in Chechnya, and was not disappointed. China happily joined for similar reasons. Turkey was the first country to offer troops for the new phase of the U.S. "war on terror," in gratitude, as the Prime Minister explained, for the U.S. contribution to Turkey's campaign against its miserably-repressed Kurdish population, waged with extreme savagery and relying crucially on a huge flow of U.S. arms. [...]

More democratic societies, including the United States, instituted measures to impose discipline on the domestic population and to institute unpopular measures under the guise of "combating terror," exploiting the atmosphere of fear and the demand for "patriotism" - which in practise means: "You shut up and I'll pursue my own agenda relentlessly." The Bush administration used the opportunity to advance its assault against most of the population, and future generations, in service to the narrow corporate interests that dominate the administration to an extent even beyond the norm.

In brief, initial predictions were amply confirmed.

One major outcome is that the United States, for the first time, has major military bases in Central Asia. These are important to position U.S. multinationals favorably in the current "great game" to control the considerable resources of the region, but also to complete the encirclement of the world's major energy resources, in the Gulf region. [...]

The Bush administration perceives the new phase of the "war on terror" (which in many ways replicates the "war on terror" declared by the Reagan administration 20 years earlier) as an opportunity to expand its already overwhelming military advantages over the rest of the world, and to move on to other methods to ensure global dominance. [...]

Vocabulary

6 ominous (adj.): making you feel that s.th. bad is going to happen - **7 atrocity** (n.): an extremely cruel and violent action, especially during a war - **8 historic** (adj.): very important and recorded as memorable event in history - regrettable (adj.): sad, unfortunate - **12 to retain** (v. fml.): to keep s.th., to continue to have s.th. - **13 preponderance** (n.): dominance - **13 to anticipate** (v.): to expect that s.th. will happen and be ready for it - **16 offshoot** (n.): organization, state that has derived from an earlier one, new stem or branch on a plant - **16 to subject** (v., fml.): /səbˈdʒekt/ to force s.o. to experience s.th. very unpleasant or painful - **16 soil** (n.): earth - **19 to disregard** (v.): to ignore - **22 repercussion** (n.): effect, consequence - **22 significant** (adj.): important, influential - **28 to assume** (v.): to think that s.th. is true, although you do not have definite proof, to presume, to reckon - **31 intelligence** (n.): organizations gathering secret information for their government - **31 investigation** (n.): attempt to find the causes of events - **32 evidence** (n.): facts or signs that show the truth, proof - **32 perpetrator** (n.): s.o. who has done s.th. morally wrong or illegal, culprit, criminal - **34 to testify** (v.): to make a formal statement of what is true - **35 to hatch** (v.): to make a plan in secret - to implement (v.): to put plans into reality - **44 unanimous** (adj.): /juːˈnænɪməs/ agreed by everyone involved in a decision - **47 infidel** (n.): an offensive word for someone of a different or no religion - **47 to overthrow, overthrew, overthrown** (v.): to remove a leader or government from power, especially by force - **48 to impose** (v.): to force people to accept s.th. - **48 to sustain** (v.): to maintain, support - **49 to institute** (v., fml.): to introduce - **50 plaintive** (adj.): sad, high-pitched - **64 exacerbated** (adj.): /ɪgˈzæsəbeɪtɪd/ *here:* embittered, angry - **67 comforting** (adj.): making you feel less worried, unhappy, upset - **68 resentment** (n.): a feeling of anger, bitterness - **72 deficiency** (n.): /dɪˈfɪʃənsi/ lack, shortage, weakness, fault - **75 contentious** (adj.): causing a lot of argument - **81 appropriateness** (n.): correctness, suitability for a particular situation - **87 to visit s.th. upon s.o.** (v.): to punish s.o., to show s.o. your rage - **95 beyond recovery**: without hope for repair - **100 to assassinate** (v.): to kill an important person - **106 to compel** (v.): to force s.o. to do s.th. - **114 to accelerate** (v.): /əkˈseləreɪt/ to speed up, to (make) go faster - **115 preemptive** (adj.): /priˈemptɪv/ preventive or preventative, intended to stop s.th. from happening - **117 to seize upon** (v.): to take up, grab eagerly, to suddenly become very interested - **118 to escalate** (v.): to become or make worse, to increase - **118 repressive** (adj.): oppressive, controlling in a cruel way - **127 to wage** (v.): to be involved in a war, lead a war - **127 savagery** (n.): /ˈsævɪdʒəri/ extremely cruel and violent behavior - **130 domestic** (adj.): home -, within a country - **134 agenda** (n.): a list of tasks, topics that have to be dealt with - **136 assault** (n.): physical attack - **138 corporate interests** (n.): economic interests of great companies - **140 ample** (adj.): more than enough, sufficient - **146 encirclement** (n.): the process of surrounding s.th. or s.o. - **148 to perceive** (v.): to see s.th., understand s.th., think of s.th. in a particular way - **149 to replicate** (v., fml.): to repeat, to copy

AWARENESS

1 What do you think about war? Can it be a legitimate means of politics if all the other political measures have failed to settle a conflict?

COMPREHENSION

2 Point out the intention of the American scholars in their document "What we're fighting for".

3 Summarize the main points of criticism directed against American attitudes and way of life.

4 How do the writers explain the attackers' motivation?

5 Summarize the American value system in your own words.

ANALYSIS

6 The authors refer to key texts of American history. Analyze the choice of words and the rhetorical devices of the letter. Form groups and point out similarities and allusions in style and content to the individual documents explicitly mentioned.

OPINION

7 In their further theses the authors of the letter define reasons for a "just" war. Discuss the concept of a "just" war in general. Discuss its validity with reference to the *War on Terror*.

PROJECT/INTERNET RESEARCH

8 After library and Internet research, report on the history of the concept of "a just war", *bellum justum*. Use the information of "Bellum Justum", www.gavagai.de/krieg/HHD312.html, as a starting-point.

Info

Just War

Its classical criteria – according to St. Augustine – are: - declaration of war and the use of force can only be ordered by a legitimate authority; - it must have a just cause, peace must be its goal; - it is a reaction to grave public evil and should not be preemptive; – it should be led with adequate, proportional means; – it should not involve innocent people; – success has to be probable; – it has to be the last resort.

Use newspaper archives or the Internet to trace the arguments of the transatlantic debate about the intellectuals' letter "What we're fighting for". Present and assess the arguments exchanged. Links: www.americanvalues.org./html/german_statement.html. ; www.carpe.com/literaturwelt/Kultur/Politik. See also: Peter Schneider, "Debatte: Die falsche Gewissheit: Zur deutsch-amerikanischen Debatte über den gerechten 'Krieg', in: *Der Spiegel* (35/2002), pp. 168 - 170, and Jörg Lau, "Welche Freiheit? Welche Werte? Amerikanische Intellektuelle über den 'Krieg gegen den Terror' und die Einschränkung der Bürgerrechte", in: *Die Zeit* (Nr. 9, 21. Februar 2002), p. 38.

COMPREHENSION

9　Explain why 9-11 is a historic event according to Chomsky.
10　Sum up Chomsky's answers to the four "crucial questions" at the beginning of his essay.

ANALYSIS

11　Analyze the style and content of Chomsky's "Reflections" and discuss whether his article could be used as a direct reply to the American intellectuals' letter "What we're fighting for".

OPINION

12　Compile information on America's use of military violence Chomsky mentions in the text. Add more examples and present your findings (background information, reactions, results).
13　Organize a formal debate:
　　The House believes that the *War on Terror* as led by the United States of America and its allies is a legitimate and adequate response.

Noam Chomsky was born in Philadelphia on December 7, 1928. Chomsky is, above all, renowned as a scholar of linguistics. His most influential contributions were his books on "generative grammar": *Syntactic Structures and Aspects of the Theory of Syntax* (1965). With his book *Language and Mind* (1968) Chomsky leaves the limited realm of linguistic theory and applies it to psychology and brain research. Since the late 1960s Chomsky has become an established critic of American and international politics. He started with analyses of the role of intellectuals – *The Responsibility of Intellectuals* (1967), an essay in which he opposes the Vietnam War and the book *American Power* and the *New Mandarins* (1969). His fields of interest as a political writer include American society and America's global role, the process of globalization, the analysis of the Mass Media, the Middle East (his views on Israel are highly controversial), and terrorism. His Reflections on 9-11 are embedded in a comprehensive system of political thought.

18

Michael Hirsh

"We Were Wrong"

America's involvement in the Vietnam conflict both reflected the principles mentioned in the Info Box, p. 59, and altered America's image as a superpower. Americans were faced with a new experience: they lost a war and their commitment proved wrong. - Michael Hirsh, "We Were Wrong" (*Newsweek*, 17 April 1995), pp.41-43

1　**Memoirs: After nearly 30 years of silence, McNamara writes of his pain and the error of his ways**

IN ONE OF THE MORE POIGNANT MOMENTS in his new memoirs, former U.S. defense secretary Robert S. McNamara describes the day in November 1965 when
5　a Quaker, Norman Morrison, stood "within forty feet of my Pentagon window" and doused himself with a gallon jug of gasoline. With his 1-year-old daughter in his arms, Morison set himself aflame. Only at the last moment did he throw the baby to safety. Morrison's self-

1965: The faces of Johnson (left) and McNamara are eloquent of the day. It was July 27, and the president has just made his decision to launch a major ground war.

10 immolation was a turning point in the mounting anti-Vietnam War protests that changed McNamara's life forever.

Once a celebrated corporate prodigy at Ford Motor Co., McNamara became an object of vilification as the
15 war ground on. People spat at him and called him "baby burner" and "murderer" in restaurants and airports. Close friends turned on him - McNamara describes how, after dinner at her New York apartment one night, Jacqueline Kennedy "suddenly exploded. She turned and began,
20 literally, to beat on my chest, demanding that I 'do something to stop the slaughter!'" His response to all this was characteristic sang-froid. "I reacted [...] by bottling up my emotions and avoided talking about them with anyone - even my family."

25 So it has been for nearly 30 years. America, meanwhile, has gradually made its peace with the Vietnam experience, producing a slew of hit movies and best-selling books on a subject once considered too tender for popular consumption.

30 Now it is McNamara's turn. His book, *In Retrospect: The Tragedy and Lessons of Vietnam* [...] is a long wrenching mea culpa, "the book I planned never to write," he says.

In it, McNamara admits that both the Kennedy and
35 Johnson administrations simply didn't understand what they were doing in Vietnam. He says they overestimated the threat of monolithic communism, "totally underestimated the nationalist aspect of Ho Chi Minh's movement," and erred grievously by deceiving the
40 American public. "We were wrong, terribly wrong. We owe it to future generations to explain why," he writes.

No explanation: Often, however, McNamara says that he cannot explain why - not even to himself, much less to future generations. Renowned for his analytical skills,
45 he remains baffled to this day as to why he and his colleagues among "the best and the brightest" did not think realistically about the possible consequences of Vietnam. "We failed to analyze our assumptions critically, then or later," he says.

50 In a drumbeat of somber rhetoric, McNamara recounts all the times he failed to ask the right questions and ignored, under political pressure, his own better judgment about keeping combat troops out of Vietnam. The exaggerated fear of communist expansionism that ruled the era sucked the United States into Vietnam – almost
55 inevitably, it now seems – to the point at which extrication might have required a far more courageous and wiser leader than Lyndon B. Johnson, though McNamara does his best to avoid coming to this conclusion. McNamara speculates that John F. Kennedy,
60 had he lived, would have pulled America out before too long, although the assassinated president never told him what he planned to do. As evidence, McNamara points to Kennedy's refusal to commit U.S. forces to an invasion of Cuba, both during the Bay of Pigs and Cuban missile
65 crises. "Kennedy would have agreed that withdrawal would cause a fall of the 'dominoes' but that staying in would ultimately lead to the same result, while exacting a terrible price in blood," he writes.

Grasping for explanations, he often resorts to pleading
70 ignorance – "we found ourselves setting policy for a region that was terra incognita." Other times, McNamara suggests, major errors were made through the mere distraction of being too busy. He concedes that his generation of policy wonks was also overwhelmed by
75 the task of world leadership. "Our failure was partially the result of having many more commitments than just Vietnam" – among them Latin America, Europe, civil rights and the legislative program of Johnson's Great Society. "We were left harried, overburdened."
80

Whatever the reason, in the end the Johnson administration chose the worst possible policy course in Vietnam: it failed to ask for a declaration of war and thereby ensure popular and congressional support; instead it secretly struck a dithering compromise. It took the
85 middle road between withdrawing to appease the left and escalating up to total war - or invading North Vietnam - to satisfy the hawks. The result was a limited war without direction or well-defined goals. [...]

In the end, the book seems to suggest, 58,000 young
90 Americans went to the slaughter to help Lyndon Johnson preserve support for his Great Society programs and to avoid looking soft on communism before the right wing.

In one of his few attempts at exculpating himself, McNamara makes no apologies for his controversial
95 decision not to speak out once he turned against the war in 1967 and came under pressure to resign as defense secretary. Though "to this day I don't know if I was fired or quit," he chose his loyalty to Johnson personally and to the presidency over his conscience and made no public
100 criticism after leaving to become president of the World Bank. He also defends himself against criticisms that he was a bloodless calculator of "body counts" – the chilling phrase that dominated headlines during Vietnam. "Things you can count, you ought to count. Loss of life
105

is one when you are fighting a war of attrition," he writes.

Perhaps the most redeeming aspect of Johnson's handling of the war, in McNamara's account, was his unwillingness to risk war with China and Russia. In what many might see as an endorsement of civilian control of the military, McNamara reveals that he and Johnson "were shocked by the almost cavalier way in which the (joint) chiefs and their associates [...] referred to, and accepted the risk of, the possible use of nuclear weapons." It was a realization that troubles him still: "I believe that even a low risk of a catastrophic event must be avoided. That lesson had not been learned in 1964. I fear neither our nation nor

The Vietnam Memorial in Washington

the world has fully learned it to this day."

He is no doubt correct. If the reformed sinner often makes the best preacher, perhaps the man who disastrously prosecuted a "limited war" is best suited to tell us how one should be fought today. But don't expect many to listen. McNamara says his main reason for writing *In Retrospect* is that he has "grown sick at heart witnessing the cynicism and even contempt with which so many people view our political institutions and leaders." His own confessions of error, while long overdue, will do little to reinvigorate the American people's faith in government.

Info

"**American foreign policy**, or the set of goals that determines America's relations with other governments and its stance on international issues, has been guided by several principles.

First, American foreign policy serves a moral aim in promoting and protecting democratic systems and democratic values such as individual freedom and human rights. This ideal is often referred to as 'making the world safe for democracy.'

Second, American policy is committed to the practical principle of protecting America's political and economic interests.

Third, American foreign policy is directed toward maintaining the balance of international power.

These three principles have guided U.S. policies since the early part of the century when the nation began playing an increasingly important role in international affairs."

(Fiedler, Jansen, Norman-Risch, America in Close-Up, Longman Group Ltd., Harlow, 1990, p.173)

Vocabulary

Intro/3 commitment (n.): the use of money, time, people, etc. for a particular purpose - **photo/1 eloquent** : showing a feeling or meaning without using words - **2 poignant** (adj.): /'pɔɪnjənt/ making you sad or full of pity - **6 to douse** (v.): to put into liquid or pour liquid over - **9 self-immolation** (n.): killing oneself for religious or political reasons, esp. by burning - **13 corporate** (adj.): of or belonging to a big company or group of companies acting together as a single organization - **13 prodigy** (n.): person who has unusual and very noticeable abilities - **14 vilification** (n.): /ˌvɪlɪfɪ'keɪʃn/ saying bad things about s.o., esp. things that are not true - **15 to grind** on (v.): to continue for an unpleasantly long time - **22 sang-froid** (n.): /ˌsɒŋ'frwɑː ‖ ˌsɑːŋ-/ (French for "cold blood") courage and the ability to keep calm in dangerous or difficult situations - **22 to bottle up** (v.): to deliberately not allow yourself to show a strong feeling or emotion - **27 slew** (n.): a large number of - **27 hit movie** (n.): an extremely popular movie - **28 tender** (adj.): sensitive - **30 in retrospect** (n.): thinking back to a time in the past, esp. with the advantage of knowing more now than you did then - **32 wrenching** (adj.): painful - **32 mea culpa** (Latin): /ˌmeɪə 'kʊlpə/ admission that s.th. is your fault - **36 to overestimate**

(v.): to guess an amount or value that is too high - **37 monolithic** (adj.): (of a political system that is) very large and powerful and difficult to change - **39 grievous** (adj.): very serious and likely to be very harmful - **39 to deceive** (v.): to make s.o. believe that s.th. is not true in order to get what you want - **44 renowned** (adj.): /rɪ'naʊnd/ known and admired by a lot of people, esp. for some special skill or s.th. that you have done - **45 baffled** (adj.): unable to understand or explain s.th. - **48 assumption** (n.): s.th. that you think is true although you have no proof - **50 drumbeat** (n.): the sound made when s.o. hits a drum - **50 somber** (adj.): sad and serious - **50 rhetoric** (n.): the art of speaking or writing - **53 combat troops** (n.): troops fighting against an enemy - **54 expansionism** (n.): a process in which the amount of land and power that a country has increases - **55 to suck** (v.): to pull s.o. or s.th. with great power or force to a particular place - **56 inevitable** (adj.): /ɪn'evɪtəbl/ certain to happen and impossible to avoid - **57 extrication** (n.): removing s.o. or s.th. from a place in which they are trapped - **62 to assassinate** (v.): to murder an important person - **68 ultimately** (adv.): after everything else has been done or considered - **68 to exact** (v.): to demand - **70 to plead** (v.)

Explanations

photo/1 Lyndon Baines Johnson: (cf. p. 17) - **1 Robert Strange McNamara**: (*1916) U.S. defense secretary during the Kennedy and Johnson administrations, resigned in 1967 - **5 Quaker**: a member of a Christian religious group called the Society of Friends. Quakers are known for their opposition to violence and war, and are active in helping other people and in education - **6 Pentagon**: (cf. p. 43) - **13 Ford Motor Co.**: American company which produces cars, set up in 1903 by Henry Ford (1863-1947) - **19 Jacqueline Kennedy**: (1929-1994): the wife of John F. Kennedy - **34 John Fitzgerald Kennedy (JFK)**: (cf. p. 17) - **39 Ho Chi Minh**: (1890-1969) Vietnamese Communist leader - **65 Bay of Pigs**: a bay on the south coast of Cuba. In 1961, a group of Cuban exiles supported by the U.S. landed in the Bay of Pigs, in an attempt to end the rule of Fidel Castro (*1927; President of Cuba). The invasion failed and all of the invading army were either taken prisoner or killed. This event is usually called the Bay of Pigs Invasion. - **65 Cuban missile crisis**: a dangerous situation which developed in 1962 when the Soviet Union began to build bases for nuclear missiles in Cuba. U.S. President John F. Kennedy complained and stopped ships from going to Cuba, and the Soviet Union agreed to remove the bases. - **79 Johnson's Great Society**: the goal of the Democratic Party during the administration of President Lyndon B. Johnson to enact programs to improve education, provide medical care for old people, reduce poverty, etc. - **101 World Bank**: (also International Bank for Reconstruction and Development) a United Nation organization which lends money for development purposes and gives technical help to governments doing large-scale projects - **117 joint chiefs**: (Joint Chiefs of Staff) the group of leaders of the four main divisions of the American army - **photo** (p. 59): Vietnam War Memorial: a structure of polished black stone in the shape of a "V" which is sunk into the ground in the park area near the Lincoln Memorial in Washington, DC. The names of the 58,000 soldiers killed in the Vietnam War are on the stone walls.

ignorance (n.): to give lack of knowledge or information about s.th. as an excuse for your actions - **72 terra incognita** (Latin): an unknown or unexplored land or region - **74 to concede** (v.): to admit that s.th. is true although you wish it was not true - **75 wonk** (n.): s.o. who works hard and is very serious - **80 harried** (adj.): worried or annoyed continually - **85 to strike** (v.): to reach; to arrive at - **85 dithering** (adj.): /ˈdɪðərɪŋ/ uncertain; indecisive - **86 to appease** (v.): to make s.o. less angry or stop them from attacking you by giving them what they want - **87 to escalate** (v.): (of war) to make or become more serious by stages - **88 hawk** (n.): /hɔːk ‖ hɒːk/ a person who believes in strong action or the use of force, esp. one who supports warlike political ideas - **94 to exculpate o.s.** (v.): to free oneself from blame - **96 to speak out** (v.): to speak bravely and openly, esp. after remaining silent for some time - **103 bloodless** (adj.): lacking human feeling - **107 war of attrition** (n.): a war in which you try to weaken and destroy the enemy by continually attacking him - **108 redeeming** (adj.): making (s.th. bad) less bad - **113 endorsement** (n.): expression of approval or support - **116 cavalier** (adj.): thoughtless and disrespectful - **128 to prosecute** (v.): to continue steadily (s.th. that needs effort) - **137 overdue** (adj.): /ˌəʊvəˈdjuː/ not having been done at the required or appropriate time - **138 to reinvigorate** (v.): /ˌriːɪnˈvɪɡəreɪt/ to give freshness or strength to s.o. or s.th. again

Info

Vietnam War (1954-1975)

A long civil war in Vietnam between the North and the South. The government of the South, in Saigon, was helped by the U.S. and other countries to fight against the Viet Cong, guerrillas (= unofficial soldiers) who were supported by the Communist government of the North. The South was unsuccessful even with U.S. help. Many people in the West associate the war in Vietnam with the strong public protest against it. While half a million American soldiers were fighting in Vietnam, protest marches were common at home. Protest songs included the words, "hell no, we won't go!" and the saying "make love, not war" became popular. Some young men refused to go to war for moral reasons. While some were allowed to become legal conscientious objectors, others, called draft dodgers, either left the country or went to jail in protest. Many Americans protested when they saw horrific pictures of the war dead shown on television. Others objected that the soldiers who were drafted (= made to go to war) were often poor or black, while wealthier whites could find ways to avoid the draft. When President Nixon finally brought the American forces home in 1973, they were not cheered in the streets for their courage, and they were sometimes treated badly by people who were against the war. Many people now believe that the U.S. should never have entered the war at all, for both moral and military reasons. Others still believe that the U.S. could have helped the South to win.

From: Longman Dictionary of English Language and Culture *(Longman Group Ltd., Harlow, 1992)*

1 When the Vietnam War is mentioned, what comes to your mind?
Have you heard or read anything about this military conflict?
Have you seen any of the various films dealing with this topic?
The following Internet source might be used for detailed information on Vietnam war films:
http:xx members.aol.com/warlib/10viet.htm

COMPREHENSION

2 What happened outside Robert McNamara's Pentagon office one day in November 1965?
3 A great number of people were critical of McNamara's role during the Vietnam War. How did they express their opinions?
4 What explanations does McNamara offer to point out why America became involved in the Vietnam conflict and why so many major errors were made? Are there any excuses?
5 In what way does McNamara blame himself personally for the failure of the American policy course in Vietnam?
6 Why is McNamara so critical of the role played by the U.S. military leaders?

ANALYSIS

7 In what way is the article typical of a news magazine? Analyze its layout and the way the author has structured its content.
8 Explain the images used in the following expressions:
I. 22 "bottling up my emotions"   I. 50 "in a drumbeat of somber rhetoric"
I. 67 "a fall of the 'dominoes'"   I. 86 "to take the middle road"
I. 88 "to satisfy the hawks"   I. 93 "to look soft on something"
I. 116 "the almost cavalier way"   I. 126 "the reformed sinner often makes the best preacher"
9 The cartoon (p. 60) deals with the Vietnam of 1995. What is the cartoonist's message concerning America's foreign policy?

OPINION

10 Public admission of guilt could help restore a people's confidence in government and politicians. What do you think about this statement?
11 After the end of the Soviet Union and the emergence of several independent states in its place, America's foreign policy needs a new definition. In what way should it be altered?

PROJECT

12 Working in groups, find out about other examples of U.S. interventions abroad after the Vietnam War. To what extent were these international commitments in accordance with the principles of American foreign policy mentioned in the Info Box on p. 59?

19

John Maggs

"Too Much Like Vietnam"

"The most significant parallels may be not what is happening on the battlefield, but what is happening in America". - (John Maggs, "Too Much Like Vietnam" (National Journal; Nov 22, 2003; 35, 47/48; Academic Research Library), pp. 3568-3571.

1 In many ways, the U.S. occupation of Iraq is nothing like America's decade-long war in Vietnam. In Iraq, the U.S. is facing no foe resembling the North Vietnamese army, with its tanks, home territory, and hundreds of thousands of well-trained troops. Iraq's guerillas, by contrast, aren't 5 supplied and reinforced by two nuclear-armed powers.

The resistance springs not from idealism, or even much of an ideology - it's just a yearning for a restoration of power. Most Iraqis hate or at best distrust the Saddam loyalists behind the opposition to American rule. Most U.S. military leaders with experience in both conflicts reject the comparison to Vietnam.

But the toting up of these differences misses the point. The real question is whether Iraq is enough like Vietnam to matter - whether the similarities are sufficient to give us pause and inform our outlook. Many people reject the Iraq-Vietnam comparison because they say that Iraq is not a lost cause. Based on everything we know now, it certainly isn't. But that, too, is the wrong question, because the conflict is less than a year old and far from over. Those who label every comparison to Vietnam as Vietnam-Syndrome defeatism engage in exactly the kind of Panglossianism that prevented America and its leaders from seeing what was really happening in Southeast Asia.

Vietnam was a war that was lost less on the battlefield than at home, where opposition to the war made winning it impossible. The guerrilla war now under way in Iraq bears many important similarities to Vietnam, but the more-significant parallels may be in what is happening in America. [...]

As with Vietnam, political support for Iraq has proved to be fragile in part because it was secured by a justification that has been discredited - that Iraq was intent on acquiring and probably on the verge of deploying chemical, biological, and nuclear weapons that would threaten U.S. interests. President Bush used false evidence of Iraq's nuclear ambitions to justify a vote last fall authorizing the war; Lyndon Johnson knowingly misused false reports on an attack on U.S. ships to justify the 1964 Gulf of Tonkin resolution, which cleared the way for a large deployment of ground troops. Critics of the Iraq war say that the willful twisting of facts, the exploitation of America's fear and grief over 9/11, and the badgering of politicians and reporters who challenge these tactics all echo the mistakes that U.S. leaders made during Vietnam. [...]

Frederik Longevall, author of *The Origins of the Vietnam War,* said that one striking similarity between Iraq and Vietnam is the unusual lack of international support for both campaigns. "You saw almost all our allies saying that Vietnam was a mistake, and when we ignored that advice, we were on our own, and there was some damage to U.S. influence," said Longevall. Then as now, the lonely support of Britain was crucial: "I think, without Britain, the U.S. would have never gone" to Vietnam. [...]

By and large, today's soldiers are better-prepared and more committed than their predecessors. That's a valid point - if you compare the troops in the early stages of the Iraq occupation to the dispirited troops who filled the ranks in the final years of the Vietnam War. In the early days of Vietnam, however, American troops were highly motivated, and they remained so until disillusionment began to creep in after 1966. In Iraq, where morale isn't uniform, the same deterioration may occur. Take, for example, the 40,000 to 50,000 military reservists who were notified recently that their tour could be extended for up to two years. As the Bush administration seeks to bring home the longest-serving enlisted personnel to stave off a loss of morale, those replacing them may be less professional, or less committed - just as in Vietnam. Until a year or two ago, reservists could expect to never see combat, let alone the shooting gallery they face in Iraq. Morale became an acute problem in Vietnam, and the administration today is acting worried that it could become a problem in Iraq.

Likewise, it is naive to assume that idealism and nationalism aren't part of what motivates the Iraqi resistance, just as they inspired the Vietnamese. The willingness of some Iraqis to launch suicide attacks should be sufficient testament to the contrary. The administration's effort to dismiss these insurgents as "thieves and murderers" is simplistic. Predictions that the guerillas would quickly disperse after the toppling of the Saddam regime were as wrong as Vietnam-era predictions that the Vietcong would flee from superior American firepower and braver American soldiers.

Don Obersdorfer did several tours in Vietnam as a reporter for the Washington Post, and he sees one overarching similarity. "What is most reminiscent of Vietnam and most disturbing is that the United States is dealing with another country with which it has no historical experience, no familiarity with the culture, and even very few people who speak the language," said Obersdorfer, who now teaches at Johns Hopkins University. This lack of understanding helps explain why the coalition has so consistently underestimated the challenges of occupation. Obersdorfer remembers when U.S. officials helped write a constitution and stage elections in South Vietnam, resulting in a government "with absolutely no legitimacy, because we never figured out what people wanted." [...]

Although it is hard to imagine the people of Iraq opposing U.S. occupation as strongly as did the peasants of South Vietnam, the tide seems to be turning. Even in the supposedly peaceful Shiite areas of southern Iraq, many local leaders oppose the occupation and yearn for an alliance with Iran. [...]

In a Gallup Poll conducted before the Ramadan offensive and released after it began, 54 percent of Americans disapproved of the job President Bush was doing in Iraq, up from a low 21 percent at the war's start. It was the first time that Bush's disapproval ratings on Iraq had exceeded 50 percent. Just as demoralizing for the White House, perhaps, was Gallup's observation that the polling resembles no other wartime experience more

than that of "the war recent presidents have avoided repeating - Vietnam." In February 1968, in the last poll
120 before Lyndon Johnson announced he wouldn't run for re-election, 57 percent of the public disapproved of his handling of Vietnam. The next poll may show Bush beyond this mark.

The most apparent and significant similarity between
125 Iraq and Vietnam is the difficulty of convincing Americans that the fight is worthwhile. First by asserting an unsubstantiated link to the war on terror and then by soft-pedaling problems in Iraq, Bush, like Johnson, has created a "credibility gap," said Stanley Karnow, "by
130 giving the impression that he is not leveling with the American people." When Bush said on October 27 that the increased violence in Iraq was a sign of progress, he reminded many of the doublespeak of Vietnam.

His unshakably positive rhetoric, the premature
135 declaration of "Mission Accomplished," the multiple and sometimes questionable justifications for war have all shaken faith in a hugely popular president. Perhaps Iraq's strongest resemblance to Vietnam lies in the unmistakable signs that Bush has heeded his shift of
140 opinion, and is responding to recent setbacks in Iraq with the dubious claim that the schedule for withdrawal should be accelerated.

In the opinion of one Vietnam veteran, this hastening would only assure a repeat of Vietnam, where the U.S. hurriedly turned security over to an ill-prepared South 145 Vietnam, withdrew U.S. troops, and then watched the regime fall a few years later. "Iraq is not Vietnam," said Sen. John McCain, R-Ariz., but "when our Secretary of Defense says that it's up to the Iraqi people to defeat the Baathists and terrorists, we send a message that America's 150 exit from Iraq is ultimately more important than the achievement of American goals."

Vocabulary

1 occupation (n.): here: when a large group of people enter a place and take control of it, esp. by military force - **3 foe** (n.): enemy - **6 to reinforce** (v.): here: to make a group of people, esp. an army, stronger by adding people, equipment, etc. - **8 yearning** (n.): a strong desire for s.th. - **13 to tote up** (v.): to add up - **18 lost cause** (n.): s.th. that has no chance of succeeding - **22 syndrome** (n.): a set of qualities, events, or types of behavior that is typical of a particular kind of problem - **22 defeatism** (n.): believing or expecting that one will not succeed - **33 fragile** (adj.): /ˈfrædʒaɪl/ ‖ -dʒəl/ a fragile situation is one that is weak or uncertain, and likely to become worse under pressure - **34 to discredit** (v.): to make people stop believing in a particular idea - **35 to acquire** (v.): to get or gain s.th. - **35 verge** (n.): to be on the verge of s.th. is to be at the point where s.th. is about to happen - **36 to deploy** (v.): to organize or move soldiers, military equipment, etc., so that they are in the righ place and ready to be used - **45 to badger** (v.): to put pressure on s.o.; to harass - **61 dispirited** (adj.): lacking hope, motivation or enthusiasm - **65 to creep in** (v.): to gradually enter s.th. and change it - **66 deterioration** (n.): /dɪˌtɪəriˈreɪʃən ‖ -ˌtɪr-/ becoming worse - **71 to stave off** (v.): to keep s.o. or s.th. from reaching you or affecting you for a period of time - **74 shooting gallery** (n.): place where people shoot guns at objects to win prizes - **82 testament** (n.): to be a testament to s.th. = proving or showing very clearly that s.th. exists or is true - **83 to dismiss** (v.): to refuse to consider s.o.'s idea, opinion, etc., because you think it is not serious, true or important - **83 insurgent** (n.): one of a group of people fighting against the government of their own country, or against authority - **85 to disperse**

(v.): to move away in different directions - **85 to topple** (v.): to take power away from a leader or government, esp. by force - **91 overarching** (adj.): including or influencing every part of s.th. - **91 reminiscent** (of) (adj.): /ˌremɪˈnɪsənt/ reminding you of s.th. - **99 to underestimate** (v.): to think or guess that s.th. is smaller, cheaper, easier, etc., than it really is - **99 challenge** (n.): s.th. that tests strength, skill or ability - **102 legitimacy** (n.): /lɪˈdʒɪtɪməsi/ the quality of being fair and reasonabe and in conformity with the law or accepted standards - **102 to figure out** (v.): to think about a problem until you find the answer or understand what has happened - **105 peasant** (n.): /ˈpezənt/ a small farmer who owns or rents a small amount of land - **106 tide** (n.): here: the way in which events or people's opinions are developing - **106 to turn** (v.): here: to change - **115 to exceed** (v.): to be more than a particular number or amount - **124 apparent** (adj): easy to notice - **126 to assert** (v.): /əˈsɜːt ‖ -ɜːrt/ to state firmly that s.th. is true - **127 unsubstantiated** (adj.): /ˌʌnsəbˈstænʃieɪtɪd/ not proved to be true - **128 to soft-pedal** (v.): to make s.th. seem less important or less urgent than it really is - **129 credibility gap** (n.): the difference between what s.o. says and what they do - **130 to level with** (v.): to speak honestly to s.o., after hiding some unpleasant facts from them - **133 doublespeak** (n.): speech that is complicated and can have more than one meaning, sometimes used deliberately to deceive or confuse people - **134 premature** (adj.): /ˈpremətʃʊə ‖ ˌpriːməˈtʃʊr/ happening before the natural or proper time - **139 to heed** (v.): to pay attention to s.o.'s advice or warning - **141 dubious** (adj.): /ˈdjuːbiəs ‖ ˈduː-/ probably not honest, right, true, etc. - **142 to accelerate** (v.): /əkˈseləreɪt/ to make s.th. take place faster

Explanations

23 Panglossiamism: The term refers to Pangloss, a character in Voltaire's novel *Candide*. Panglossianism stands for baseless optimism. - **39 Lyndon Baines Johnso**n: (cf. p. 17) - **41 Gulf of Tonkin Resolution of 1964**: The distorted account of a minor naval engagement in the Gulf of Tonkin was used by President Johnson to justify the escalation of U.S. military action in Vietnam. (cf.: www.fair.org/index.php?page=2261 and www.vietnamwar.com/GulfofTon kinResolution.htm) - **90 The Washington Post**: a serious American newspaper, printed in Washington, D.C., famous for uncovering the Watergate Scandal - **96 Johns Hopkins University**: The university in Baltimore, Maryland, opened Feb. 22, 1876. It is one of America's leading universities in both teaching and research. (cf.: www.jhu.edu/) - **107 Shiite**: a member of the second-largest branch of the Muslim religion, which is based on the teachings and acts of Muhammed's cousin Ali and of the teachers who came after him - **116 White House (the)**: (cf. p. 36) - **110 Gallup Poll**: a special count of opinions in a country, done esp. in order to try to say what the result of a political election will be, by questioning a number of people chosen to represent the whole population. They are named after the American statistician George Horace Gallup, who invented them. - **110 Ramadan**: the ninth month of the Muslim year, during which no food or drink may be taken between sunrise and sunset. - **129 Stanley Karnow**: author of "Vietnam: A History" - **135 "Mission Accomplished"**: On May 2, 2003, President Bush declared the end of major combat in Iraq aboard the aircraft carrier USS Abraham Lincoln under a banner which read "Mission Accomplished". The "Mission Accomplished" claim has been criticized and ridiculed because of the unsuccessful search for weapons of mass destruction and the continuing violence in Iraq. - **150 Baathist**: a member of a socialist political party, esp. active in Syria and Iraq

AWARENESS

1 Since the end of World War II, U.S. troops have been deployed in Germany. What do you know about the military goals that have kept American forces stationed in Germany in the course of the past 60 years?

COMPREHENSION

2 What are the main differences between the U.S. occupation of Iraq and the Vietnam War?
3 Why does the author think that significant parallels between Iraq and Vietnam may be less in what is happening on the battlefield than at home?
4 What is the international support for both campaigns like?
5 The morale of American troops became an acute problem in Vietnam. Why can the deterioration of morale become a problem in Iraq, too?
6 Why are historical experience, familiarity with the culture, and speaking the language of a foreign country so important in military commitments like Vietnam and Iraq?
7 What do opinion polls show about the American people's attitudes toward both conflicts?

ANALYSIS

8 Make a list of all the technical terms used in this text which are related to military aspects.
9 Analyze the cartoon (p. 63). Explain the message and relate it to the statements made in the article.

OPINION

10 Should the United States as the only remaining superpower after the end of the Cold War expand its military effort to defeat terrorism, prevent the development of weapons of mass destruction and/or establish democracies overseas?
11 Military force, diplomacy, international organizations like the United Nations, trade policies and economic programs could be used to achieve foreign policy goals. Discuss the efficiency and justification of the different approaches to solving international problems.

INTERNET PROJECT

12 Working in groups, find out about the widespread global U.S. troop deployment at present. As a starting point, use the material offered under www.globalsecurity.org/military/ops/global-deployments.htm.